D0561996

DAY HIKES IN
Yellowstone
NATIONAL PARK

82 GREAT HIKES

Robert Stone
4th EDITION

Day Hike Books, Inc.
RED LODGE, MONTANA

Published by Day Hike Books, Inc.
P.O. Box 865
Red Lodge, Montana 59068

Distributed by The Globe Pequot Press
246 Goose Lane
P.O. Box 480
Guilford, CT 06437-0480
800-243-0495 (direct order) · 800-820-2329 (fax order)
www.globe-pequot.com

Photographs by Robert Stone
Design by Paula Doherty

The author has made every attempt to provide accurate information in this book. However, trail routes and features may change—please use common sense and forethought, and be mindful of your own capabilities. Let this book guide you, but be aware that each hiker assumes responsibility for their own safety. The author and publisher do not assume any responsibility for loss, damage, or injury caused through the use of this book.

Cover photo: Lower Falls, Hikes 31, 32 and 34
Back cover photo: Harlequin Lake, Hike 68

Table of Contents

THE HIKES

Upper Yellowstone Park

Grand Canyon of the Yellowstone

Central Yellowstone Park to Yellowstone Lake

John D. Rockefeller Jr. Memorial Parkway

Yellowstone National Park

Yellowstone National Park is a magnificent area with beautiful, dramatic scenery and incredible hydrothermal features. Within its 2.2-million acres lies some of the earth's greatest natural treasures. An extensive network of hiking trails weaves throughout the mountains and valleys of the park. The hikes in this guide explore Yellowstone's many natural features and awe-inspiring scenery found no where else on earth.

Yellowstone was established as the world's first national park in 1872, setting the precedent for preserved lands. It is best known for Old Faithful and its many geysers. Sixty percent of the world's geysers are located in Yellowstone National Park, in addition to the more than 10,000 hot springs, bubbling mud pots, and steaming fumaroles. There are over 150 geysers located in the Upper Geyser Basin alone, making it the greatest concentration of geysers in the world. Old Faithful is located in this basin.

The park is also famous for its waterfalls and the magnificent Grand Canyon of the Yellowstone. This canyon is twenty miles long, spans 4,000 feet across, and is 1,200 feet deep. The raging Yellowstone River continues to cut through the canyon, plunging over the commanding Upper Falls (109 feet) and Lower Falls (308 feet). Several hikes explore along the rim of the canyon and down into its cavernous depths.

Yellowstone Park also has hundreds of alpine lakes. Yellowstone Lake, the headwaters to the Yellowstone River, is North America's largest mountain lake. It is over 87,000 acres, with one hundred miles of shoreline and an average depth of 139 feet.

The Continental Divide runs through the park along the perimeter of an ancient volcanic plateau. The park's center, a 28- by 47-mile caldera, is the remains of the collapsed plateau and is responsible for Yellowstone's continuing thermal activity.

Every trip to Yellowstone will include a variety of animal and nature observations. A sampling of the wildlife includes moose, bison, grizzly and black bear, elk, deer, antelope, bighorn sheep, coyote, fox, wolf, beaver, otter, chipmunk, squirrel, marmot, cutthroat trout, trumpeter swan, white pelican, osprey, owl, and bald eagle. Ecological landscapes range from near-desert vegetation to forested valleys to alpine tundra.

Day Hikes In Yellowstone National Park includes a thorough cross-section of 82 day hikes throughout the park. The hikes include all of the park's most popular attractions, as well as numerous hikes found in less traveled areas. The hikes have been chosen for their scenery, variety, geological features, and ability to be hiked within a day. All levels of hiking experience are accommodated, from level boardwalk trails to mountainous treks up to panoramic overlooks. Highlights include steep canyons, thundering waterfalls, geysers, unusual thermal features, alpine lakes, expansive meadows, and 360-degree vistas of Yellowstone Park.

A quick glance at the hikes' summaries will allow you to choose a hike that is appropriate to your ability and desire. An overall map on the next page identifies the locations of all the hikes. Several other area maps are found throughout the book. Each hike also includes its own map, driving and hiking directions, and an overview of distance/time/elevation. For further hiking into the backcountry, relevant maps are listed with each hike.

A few basic necessities will make your hike more enjoyable. Bring drinking water, snacks, hats, sunscreen, appropriate outer wear, and additional maps. Hike in supportive, comfortable shoes and wear layered clothing. Be prepared for inclement or variable weather caused by the high elevations, which range from 5,300 to 11,350 feet. Avoid surprising bison, moose, and bears by wearing a bear bell and hiking with a friend or group. Ranger stations, located at all the road junctions, have the latest information on weather, trail conditions, and animal activity.

Hiking in Yellowstone will give you a deeper appreciation of the beauty of this region and afford the opportunity to get away from the crowds. From one end of the park to the other, this area is rich in stunning landscape and diversity, scenery unrivaled from anywhere but the trails.

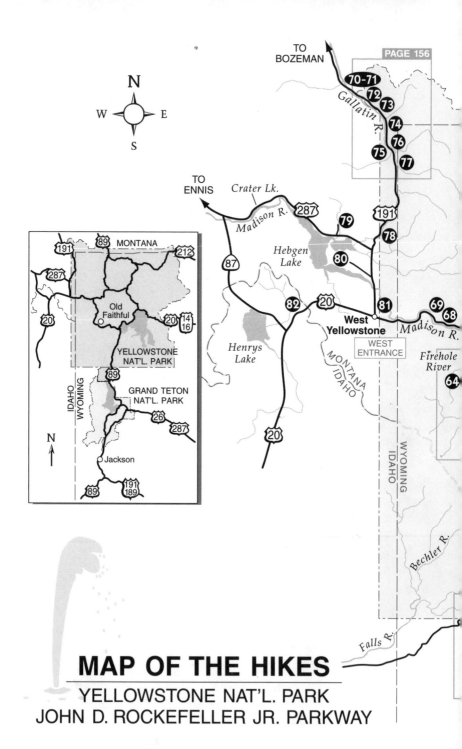

PAGE 156

TO
BOZEMAN

Gallatin R.

70-71
72
73
74
76
75
77

TO
ENNIS

Crater Lk.

Madison R.

287
79
191
78

Hebgen
Lake

87
80

82
20
81
69
68

**West
Yellowstone**

Madison R.

WEST
ENTRANCE

MONTANA
IDAHO

Firehole
River

64

Henrys
Lake

20

WYOMING
IDAHO

Bechler R.

Falls R.

N

W   E

S

89
191

MONTANA

212

287

20

Old
Faithful

20
14
16

YELLOWSTONE
NAT'L. PARK

89

GRAND TETON
NAT'L. PARK

IDAHO
WYOMING

26
287

N

Jackson

89
191
189

MAP OF THE HIKES

YELLOWSTONE NAT'L. PARK
JOHN D. ROCKEFELLER JR. PARKWAY

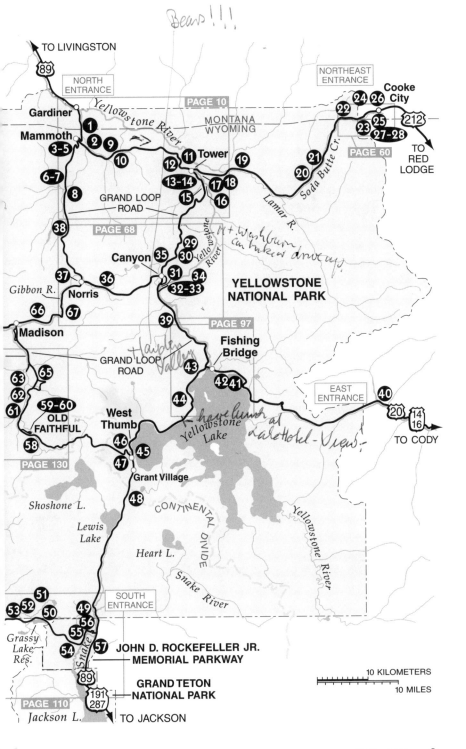

Bears!!!

TO LIVINGSTON

89

NORTH ENTRANCE

PAGE 10

NORTHEAST ENTRANCE

Cooke City

24 **26**

22

25

23

27-28

212

TO RED LODGE

Gardiner

Yellowstone River

MONTANA
WYOMING

Mammoth

1

2 **9**

3-5

6-7

10

12 **11** Tower

19

21

20

PAGE 60

8

13-14

17 **18**

Soda Butte Cr.

GRAND LOOP ROAD

15

16

38

PAGE 68

Mt. Washburn in brokers drive up

Lamar R.

29

Yellowstone River

Canyon

35

30

37

36

31

34

YELLOWSTONE NATIONAL PARK

Gibbon R.

Norris

32-33

66

67

39

PAGE 97

Fishing Bridge

Madison

GRAND LOOP ROAD

Hayden Valley

43

63

65

42 **41**

EAST ENTRANCE

40

62

44

61

59-60

OLD FAITHFUL

West Thumb

Yellowstone Lake

have lunch at Lake Hotel - Views.

20 **14** **16**

TO CODY

58

46

PAGE 130

45

47

Grant Village

Shoshone L.

48

CONTINENTAL DIVIDE

Yellowstone River

Lewis Lake

Heart L.

Snake River

51

53 **52**

50

SOUTH ENTRANCE

49

56

55

54

57

JOHN D. ROCKEFELLER JR.
MEMORIAL PARKWAY

Grassy Lake Res.

Snake

89

GRAND TETON
NATIONAL PARK

191 **287**

PAGE 110

Jackson L.

TO JACKSON

10 KILOMETERS

10 MILES

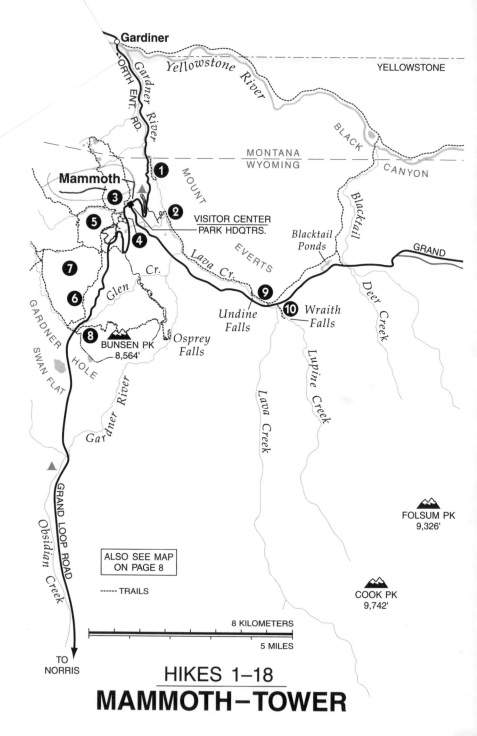

Gardiner

Yellowstone River

YELLOWSTONE

NORTH ENT. RD.

Gardner River

BLACK

CANYON

MONTANA
WYOMING

❶

MOUNT

Mammoth

❸

❷

VISITOR CENTER
PARK HDQTRS.

Blacktail

*Blacktail
Ponds*

GRAND

❺

❹

Lava Cr.

EVERTS

Cr.

❾

Deer Creek

❼

Glen

❻

*Undine
Falls*

❿ *Wraith
Falls*

GARDNER

❽ BUNSEN PK
8,564'

*Osprey
Falls*

HOLE

SWAN FLAT

Lupine Creek

Gardner River

Lava Creek

GRAND LOOP ROAD

FOLSUM PK
9,326'

Obsidian Creek

ALSO SEE MAP
ON PAGE 8

----- TRAILS

COOK PK
9,742'

8 KILOMETERS

5 MILES

TO
NORRIS

HIKES 1–18
MAMMOTH–TOWER

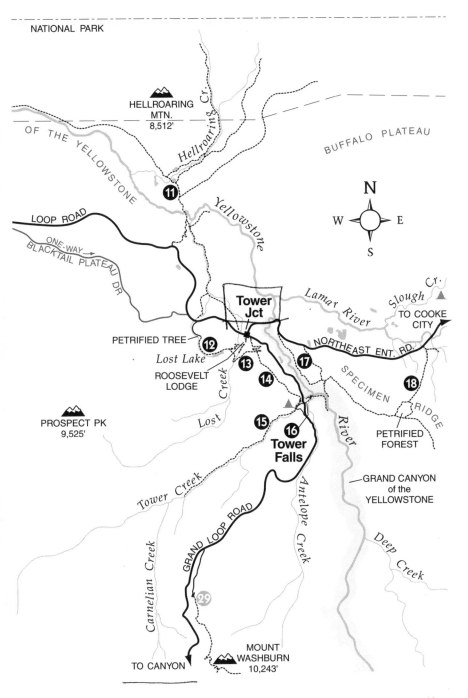

NATIONAL PARK

HELLROARING
MTN.
8,512'

Hellroaring Cr.

BUFFALO PLATEAU

OF THE YELLOWSTONE

Yellowstone

11

LOOP ROAD

ONE-WAY
BLACKTAIL PLATEAU DR

N
W   E
S

Lamar River

Slough Cr.

TO COOKE
CITY

**Tower
Jct**

PETRIFIED TREE **12**

NORTHEAST ENT. RD.

Lost Lake **13**

14

17

SPECIMEN

18

ROOSEVELT
LODGE

Lost Creek

PROSPECT PK
9,525'

Lost

15

16
**Tower
Falls**

RIDGE

PETRIFIED
FOREST

River

GRAND CANYON
of the
YELLOWSTONE

Tower Creek

GRAND LOOP ROAD

Antelope Creek

Deep Creek

Carnelian Creek

29

TO CANYON

MOUNT
WASHBURN
10,243'

Albright Visita Ctr p.52
see Mammoth Hot Springs. p. 49
David x

Hike 1
Boiling River Trail
and Swimming Hole

Hiking distance: 1.5 miles round trip
Hiking time: 50 minutes plus soaking
Elevation gain: Level
Maps: U.S.G.S. Mammoth
        Trails Illustrated Mammoth Hot Springs

Summary of hike: Boiling River is a thermal hot spring on the Gardner River that has the largest discharge of thermal water in Yellowstone. The underground hot spring flows from Mammoth Hot Springs and drops over travertine rocks into the swift current of the cool river. The hot springs mix with the river, creating a popular swimming and soaking area with hot pools, small waterfalls, and lush alpine vegetation. The trail lies on the 45th parallel, exactly half way between the equator and the North Pole. This hike is an easy trail that clings to the west bank of the Gardner River en route to the thermal soaking pools.

Driving directions: From the Mammoth Visitor Center, drive 2.3 miles north towards Gardiner to the sign which reads "45th Parallel of Latitude." Turn left or right and park in the lots on either side of the road.

Hiking directions: From the parking lot on the east side of the road, hike south on the level path. The trail heads upstream along the banks of the Gardner River on the well traveled path. The pools are easy to spot from the clouds of steam rising from the river. Across the river are the rocky slopes of the Mount Everts. While soaking, stay close to the riverbank in the rock-lined pools. Use caution not to venture into the cold, fast moving river current.

    A longer hike to the pools begins from the Mammoth Campground and heads northeast, dropping 300 feet down to the river.

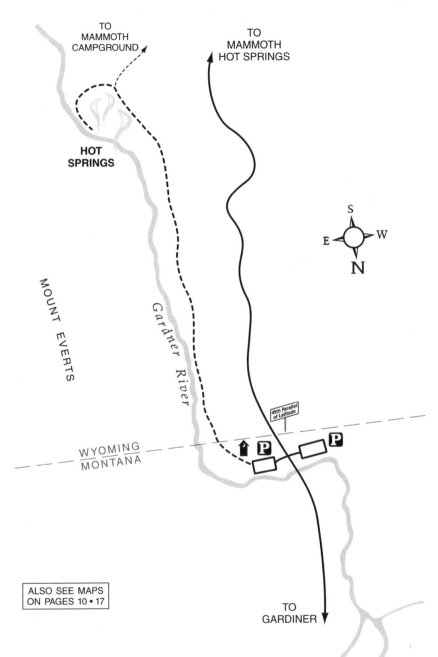

TO
MAMMOTH
CAMPGROUND

TO
MAMMOTH
HOT SPRINGS

**HOT
SPRINGS**

S

E ⊙ W

N

MOUNT EVERTS

Gardner River

45th Parallel
of Latitude

P

P

WYOMING
MONTANA

ALSO SEE MAPS
ON PAGES 10 • 17

TO
GARDINER

BOILING RIVER TRAIL
AND SWIMMING HOLE

Hike 2
Lava Creek Trail to Undine Falls

Hiking distance: 6 miles round trip
Hiking time: 3 hours
Elevation gain: 500 feet
Maps: U.S.G.S. Mammoth
Trails Illustrated Mammoth Hot Springs

Summary of hike: Undine Falls is a three-tiered waterfall on Lava Creek between Mammoth and Tower. The falls drops more than 100 feet over the cliffs of a basalt lava flow at the head of Lava Creek Canyon. The cataract drops off the cliff ledge, shoots up, and fans out to twice the width before hitting another ledge and dropping straight down. The upper portion of the waterfall can be viewed from a pullout along the road on the south rim of the canyon. The forested Lava Creek Trail leads to the falls on the opposite (north) side of the canyon, away from the crowds. The falls can be reached from two directions. The shorter 2-mile round trip hike begins at the Lava Creek picnic area near the Lava Creek Bridge (Hike 9). This hike, the longer route, begins at Mammoth and follows the Gardner River and Lava Creek up canyon to the dramatic falls.

Driving directions: From the Mammoth Visitor Center, drive 0.9 miles north towards Gardiner to a road on the right with a sign which says "Residential Area." Turn right. Drive 0.2 miles, winding around a school, to a road on the left with a sign that says "service road." Continue on the left road 0.6 miles to the trailhead pullout on the right.

Hiking directions: From the parking pullout, the trail leads toward the Gardner River. It winds around the hill to a bridge spanning the river. After crossing, continue to the right, following the river upstream. The trail continues along Lava Creek, while the Gardner River heads to the south. As you near Undine Falls, the trail climbs to the top of the cliffs for a tremendous view of the falls. There are log crossings past the falls that lead to the Undine Falls Overlook on the other side. Many hikers cross the logs, but it is dangerous and not advised. You may also continue a half mile southeast on the Lava Creek Trail to a junction with the Howard Eaton Trail. (En route, a side path on the right leads to the brink of the falls in a Douglas fir forest.) The right fork leads to the Lava Creek picnic area (Hike 9). To return, take the same trail down the canyon back to the parking pullout.

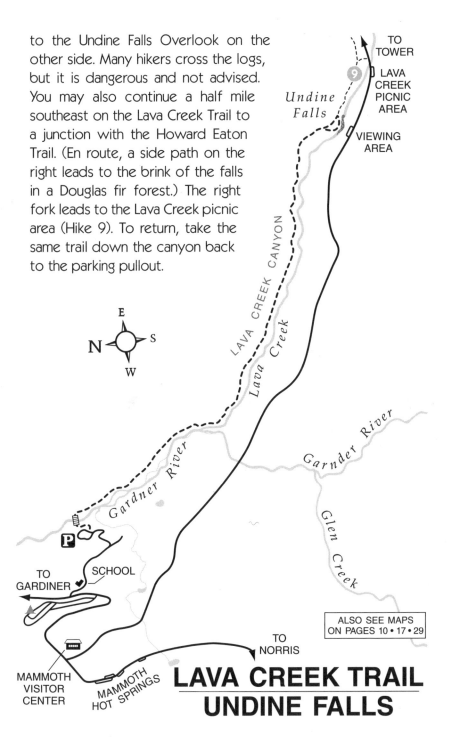

TO TOWER

LAVA CREEK PICNIC AREA

Undine Falls

VIEWING AREA

LAVA CREEK CANYON

Lava Creek

E
N — S
W

Gardner River

Garnder River

Glen Creek

Gardner River

P

TO GARDINER

SCHOOL

ALSO SEE MAPS ON PAGES 10 • 17 • 29

TO NORRIS

MAMMOTH VISITOR CENTER

MAMMOTH HOT SPRINGS

LAVA CREEK TRAIL
UNDINE FALLS

Hike 3
Beaver Ponds Loop

Hiking distance: 5 mile loop
Hiking time: 2.5 hours
Elevation gain: 550 feet
Maps: U.S.G.S. Mammoth
       Trails Illustrated Mammoth Hot Springs

Summary of hike: The Beaver Ponds Loop leads to a series of active beaver ponds on the Montana–Wyoming border. The trail passes through a diverse cross section of landscapes, including open rolling hills with grassy meadows, sagebrush plateaus, a shaded stream-fed gulch, Douglas fir and Engelmann spruce forests, aspen groves, scenic overlooks with panoramic vistas, beaver ponds in wetland meadows, and numerous small streams and footbridges.

Driving directions: From the Mammoth Visitor Center, drive 0.3 miles south towards Norris to Mammoth Hot Springs Lower Terraces. Park in the lots on either side of the road.

Hiking directions: The trailhead is on the north side of the Mammoth Terraces by the bus parking lot next to Clematis Creek. Hike west between Liberty Cap and the stone house on the Sepulcher/Beaver Ponds Trail, crossing a footbridge over the creek. Head up Clematis Gulch to a junction with the Howard Eaton Trail on the left (Hike 5). Take the right fork, recrossing Clematis Creek and continuing up the gulch. At 0.7 miles, the trail curves north to a signed junction with the Sepulcher Mountain Trail (also Hike 5). Go right on the Beaver Ponds Trail to a ridge overlooking Mammoth, Sheep Mountain, and Mount Everts. Continue north along the ridge, ducking in and out of the forest and across a wooden bridge. At 2.4 miles the trail descends to the first pond. After the third pond, the trail crosses four bridges and several small streams. At the north end of the trail, follow a stream through grassy meadows, and head south along the shoreline of a large pond. Cross the outlet stream by a beaver dam, and weave through the forest to a plateau covered in sagebrush, known as Elk Plaza. Return along the plateau, with views of Gardiner, the Absaroka Mountains, Sepulcher Mountain, Mount Everts, and Bunsen Peak. Descend down to Mammoth by the hotel.

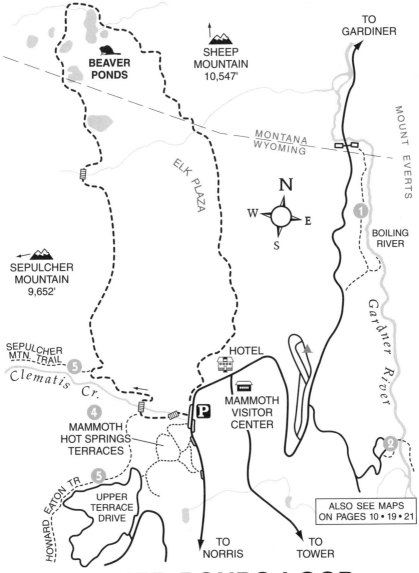

BEAVER PONDS LOOP

Hike 4
Mammoth Hot Springs
Terrace Trails

Hiking distance: 1 mile round trip
Hiking time: 1 hour
Elevation gain: 300 feet
Maps: U.S.G.S. Mammoth
   Trails Illustrated Mammoth Hot Springs
   Yellowstone Association Mammoth Hot Springs map

Summary of hike: Mammoth Hot Springs are magnificent travertine terraces formed by mineral laden hot water, limestone, and carbon dioxide. The many colors of these terraces are from living bacteria and algae. These colors change at different temperatures. White and yellow are the hottest. As the water cools, brown, green, and orange algae take hold. The mineral formations are shaped by flowing water from the springs and ground slope. These landscapes are in constant evolving motion. This hike follows a series of walkways and boardwalks that loop around and through the terraces. If you have an opportunity to visit in the winter, you will witness these hot springs at their best.

Driving directions: From the Mammoth Visitor Center, drive 0.3 miles south on the Grand Loop Road towards Norris. The terraces are easily visible. There are parking lots located on both sides of the road.

Hiking directions: From the parking lot, hike towards Liberty Cap, an extinct hot spring cone that stands out like a giant monolith at the start of the trail. There are various routes to take. They all loop around and interconnect throughout the lower terraces. Boardwalk trails link the Upper and Lower Terraces. Choose your own route. Be sure to drive the upper terrace loop, which enters a forested area. During the winter this road is a wonderful cross-country ski trail.

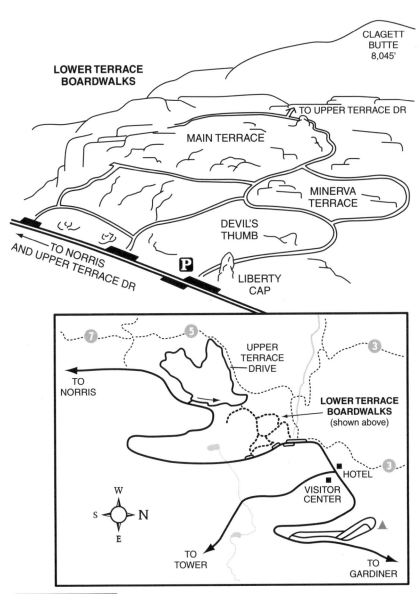

CLAGETT
BUTTE
8,045'

LOWER TERRACE
BOARDWALKS

TO UPPER TERRACE DR

MAIN TERRACE

MINERVA
TERRACE

DEVIL'S
THUMB

TO NORRIS
AND UPPER TERRACE DR

P

LIBERTY
CAP

⑦   ⑤

UPPER
TERRACE
DRIVE

③

TO
NORRIS

LOWER TERRACE
BOARDWALKS
(shown above)

③

HOTEL

VISITOR
CENTER

W
S ✦ N
E

TO
TOWER

TO
GARDINER

ALSO SEE MAPS
ON PAGES 10 • 17 • 21

MAMMOTH HOT SPRINGS
TERRACE TRAILS

Hike 5
Clagett Butte—Snow Pass Loop

Hiking distance: 4.6 mile loop
Hiking time: 2.5 hours
Elevation gain: 1,100 feet
Maps: U.S.G.S. Mammoth
　　　　 Trails Illustrated Mammoth Hot Springs

Summary of hike: This hike has several diverse landscapes, including a shaded stream-fed gulch; a Douglas fir and Engelmann spruce forest; an open plateau with views of Sepulcher Mountain, Terrace Mountain, and Bunsen Peak; ponds; fissures; and an active thermal terrace. The loop trail begins at the Mammoth Hot Spring Terraces and climbs through Clematis Creek Canyon en route to Snow Pass. The hike returns through Pinyon Terrace and an array of thermal features on Narrow Gauge Terrace.

Driving directions: From the Mammoth Visitor Center, drive 0.3 miles south towards Norris to the Mammoth Hot Springs Lower Terraces. Park in the lots on either side of the road.

Hiking directions: Walk around the north (right) side of the Mammoth Terraces between Liberty Cap and the stone house on the Sepulcher/Beaver Ponds Trail. Follow Clematis Creek upstream, and cross a wooden bridge to the south side of the creek. At 0.2 miles is a second bridge crossing and a junction with the Howard Eaton Trail (the return route). Begin the loop to the right, recrossing the bridge over Clematis Creek. Climb steadily up Clematis Canyon along the watercourse. Climb two switchbacks out of the canyon to the hillside and a junction at 0.7 miles. The right fork leads to the Beaver Ponds (Hike 3). Take the Sepulcher Mountain Trail to the left, continuing uphill above the creek to a junction at 1.5 miles. Leave the Sepulcher Mountain Trail, and bear left on the Clagett Butte Trail, climbing a short distance. Cross a wooden bridge over Clematis Creek and leave the creek, passing a tree-lined pond on the right and another on the left. Zigzag up the hillside, reaching the high point of the hike on an exposed sage-covered plateau at 2 miles. Reenter the forest and descend to the Snow Pass Trail at 2.6 miles (Hike 7). Take the left fork downhill, passing a deep, unmarked fissure on the right, to the signed Howard Eaton Trail at 3.3 miles. The right fork leads to The Hoodoos (Hike 6) and Bunsen Peak (Hike 8). Take the left fork and stay to the left at an unsigned trail split. Wind through the Narrow Gauge Terrace, a thermal area along the base of the hillside, past the Mammoth Upper Terraces. Complete the loop at Clematis Creek. Return to the right.

TERRACE MTN 8,006'

SNOW PASS

CLAGETT BUTTE 8,045'

CLAGETT BUTTE TR

TO SEPULCHER MOUNTAIN

SEPULCHER MTN TRAIL

W
S — N
E

POWER POLES

Clematis Creek

FISSURE

PINYON TERRACE

TO HOODOOS (HIKE 6)

HOWARD EATON TRAIL

NARROW GAUGE TERRACE

TO NORRIS

UPPER TERRACE DRIVE

TO BEAVER PONDS (HIKE 3)

MAMMOTH HOT SPRINGS

ALSO SEE MAPS ON PAGES 10 • 17 • 19 • 25

P

HOTEL

TO TOWER

VISITOR CENTER

CLAGETT BUTTE– SNOW PASS LOOP

TO GARDINER

Hike 6
The Hoodoos

Hiking distance: 3 miles round trip
Hiking time: 1.5 hours
Elevation gain: 400 feet
Maps: U.S.G.S. Mammoth
       Trails Illustrated Mammoth Hot Springs

Summary of hike: The Hoodoos are odd-shaped travertine limestone formations standing like statues in a large rock garden. The sculpted rocks were formed by ancient hot spring deposits high above on Terrace Mountain, which then tumbled down the mountain's east face in a large landslide. This hike follows the eastern slope of Terrace Mountain to the Hoodoos.

Driving directions: The Hoodoos are located on the road between Mammoth and Norris. From Mammoth, drive 4.7 miles south to the Glen Creek Trailhead parking lot on the left, just after crossing the Golden Gate Bridge. From Norris, drive 16.2 miles north towards Mammoth to the Glen Creek Trailhead parking lot on the right.

Hiking directions: Cross the park road and take the signed Glen Creek Trail west across the grassy meadow. Cross a wooden bridge over the meandering Glen Creek to a signed junction at 0.2 miles. Take the Howard Eaton Trail to the right through the forested terrain and up to a ridge. Traverse the cliffside along the east edge of Terrace Mountain, heading north. At 1.3 miles the path enters the Hoodoos. Stroll through this incredible display of rocks to the end of the formations. This is our turnaround spot. Return by retracing your route.

To hike further, the Howard Eaton Trail continues to Mammoth. Or, for a 6.2-mile loop hike, continue with Hike 7, circling Terrace Mountain via Snow Pass.

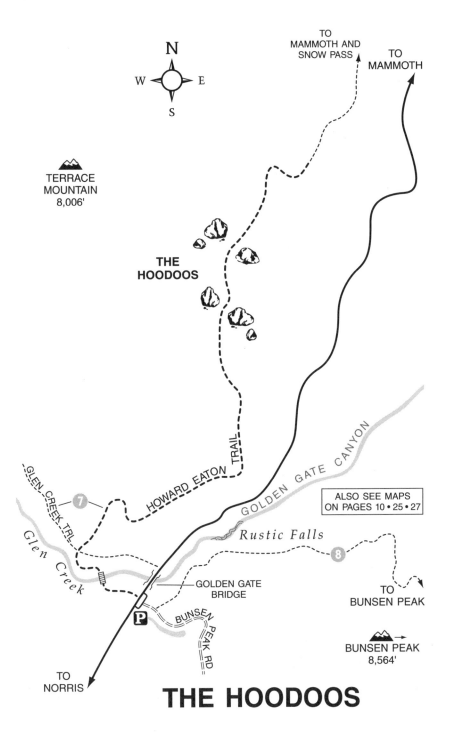

N

W · E

S

TO
MAMMOTH AND
SNOW PASS

TO
MAMMOTH

TERRACE
MOUNTAIN
8,006'

THE
HOODOOS

HOWARD EATON TRAIL

GOLDEN GATE CANYON

GLEN CREEK TRL.

7

ALSO SEE MAPS
ON PAGES 10 • 25 • 27

Rustic Falls

8

Glen Creek

GOLDEN GATE
BRIDGE

TO
BUNSEN PEAK

P

BUNSEN PEAK RD.

BUNSEN PEAK
8,564'

TO
NORRIS

THE HOODOOS

Hike 7
Terrace Mountain Loop

Hiking distance: 6.2 mile loop
Hiking time: 3 hours
Elevation gain: 600 feet
Maps: U.S.G.S. Mammoth
          Trails Illustrated Mammoth Hot Springs

Summary of hike: The Terrace Mountain Loop circles the base of Terrace Mountain through a diverse landscape. The hike weaves through the Hoodoos, a garden of dynamic travertine rock formations (Hike 6). The north end of the loop crosses Pinyon Terrace and Snow Pass between Terrace Mountain and Clagett Butte. The return route follows Glen Creek through Gardners Hole, an expansive grassland meadow.

Driving directions: Same as Hike 6.

Hiking directions: Cross the park road, picking up the signed Glen Creek Trail. Cross the meadow and a bridge to a signed junction at 0.2 miles. Bear right on the Howard Eaton Trail through the forested terrain, curving east to a ridge directly across from Bunsen Peak. Head north, following the cliffside through the Hoodoos, a dramatic garden of travertine boulders. Past the formations, follow the rolling hills through meadows, aspens, and pine groves to a signed junction at 2.6 miles. The trail straight ahead leads to Mammoth (Hike 5). Take the trail to the left towards Snow Pass. Watch for a deep fissure on the left 0.3 miles from the junction. Cross Pinyon Terrace, passing a junction with the Clagett Butte Trail on the right (Hike 5). Continue west through Snow Pass along the base of Clagett Butte, parallel to power poles. Cross the narrow pass past a kidney-shaped pond on the left tucked into a bowl. Curve around the pond to a saddle and descend along the north edge of the meadow. Cross under the power lines and bear left on a double-track trail. Head south along the west edge of Terrace Mountain, returning through the valley on the Glen Creek Trail.

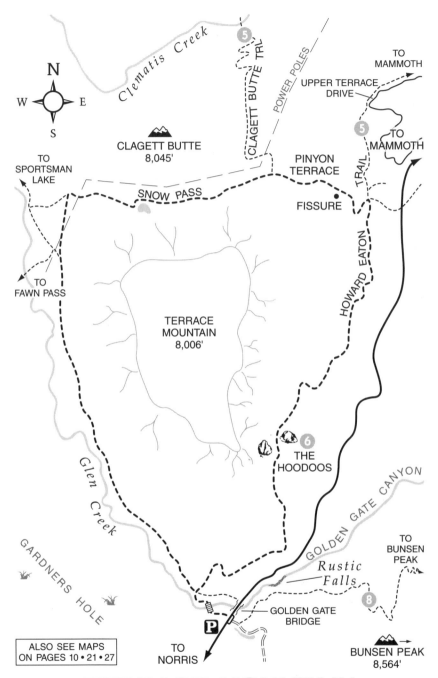

N
W E
S

Clematis Creek

CLAGETT BUTTE
8,045'

⑤

CLAGETT BUTTE TRL

POWER POLES

TO MAMMOTH

UPPER TERRACE
DRIVE

⑤

TO MAMMOTH

PINYON
TERRACE

FISSURE

HOWARD EATON TRAIL

TO SPORTSMAN
LAKE

SNOW PASS

TO FAWN PASS

TERRACE
MOUNTAIN
8,006'

Glen Creek

THE
HOODOOS ⑥

GOLDEN GATE CANYON

TO BUNSEN
PEAK

GARDNERS HOLE

Rustic Falls

⑧

GOLDEN GATE
BRIDGE

Ⓟ

TO NORRIS

BUNSEN PEAK
8,564'

ALSO SEE MAPS
ON PAGES 10 • 21 • 27

TERRACE MOUNTAIN

Hike 8
Bunsen Peak

Hiking distance: 4.4 miles round trip
Hiking time: 2 hours
Elevation gain: 1,345 feet
Maps: U.S.G.S. Mammoth
Trails Illustrated Mammoth Hot Springs

Summary of hike: Dome-shaped Bunsen Peak is the eroded remains of a volcanic cone that rises to the northeast of Swan Lake Flat. From the top of Bunsen Peak are incredible views, including Mount Holmes to the southwest; Gardners Hole, the Gallatin Range, and Electric Peak to the west; Cathedral Rock, the Mammoth Terraces, and the Absaroka Range to the north; and the Washburn Range to the east. The trail to the peak winds through a burned Douglas fir and lodgepole pine forest from the 1988 fires. A beautiful new-growth forest has carpeted the hillsides.

Driving directions: From Mammoth, drive 4.7 miles south to the Glen Creek Trailhead parking lot on the left, just after crossing Golden Gate Bridge. From Norris, drive 16.2 miles north towards Mammoth to the Glen Creek Trailhead parking lot on the right.

Hiking directions: Walk twenty yards up the gated, unpaved Bunsen Peak Road to the signed Bunsen Peak Trail on the left. Head northeast on the footpath, winding up the hillside while viewing Bunsen Peak to the east. The trail levels out through a burned area, then climbs a slope to a saddle. Views open up of Gardners Hole, Swan Lake, and the Gallatin Range to the south and west. Begin the steep ascent to the peak. A short distance ahead, switchbacks zigzag up the west slope of the mountain, minimizing the steep grade. Near the top, the trail passes radio relay equipment and heads south to the peak. After enjoying the views, return along the same path.

To hike further, the trail continues 1.8 miles east down the mountain and joins Bunsen Peak Road less than one mile from Osprey Falls.

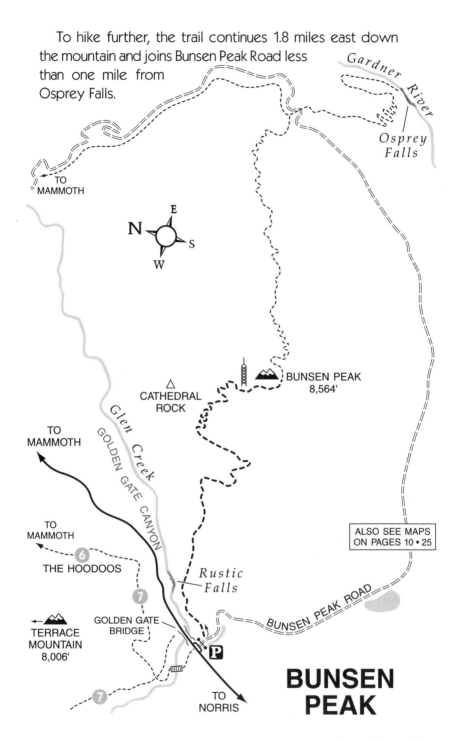

Gardner River

Osprey
Falls

TO
MAMMOTH

N
E
S
W

BUNSEN PEAK
8,564'

△
CATHEDRAL
ROCK

Glen Creek

GOLDEN GATE CANYON

TO
MAMMOTH

TO
MAMMOTH

6
THE HOODOOS

7

*Rustic
Falls*

ALSO SEE MAPS
ON PAGES 10 • 25

BUNSEN PEAK ROAD

TERRACE
MOUNTAIN
8,006'

GOLDEN GATE
BRIDGE

P

7

TO
NORRIS

BUNSEN
PEAK

Hike 9
Undine Falls
from the Lava Creek Picnic Area

Hiking distance: 2 miles round trip
Hiking time: 40 minutes
Elevation gain: 50 feet
Maps: U.S.G.S. Mammoth and Blacktail Deer Creek
        Trails Illustrated Mammoth Hot Springs

Summary of hike: Undine Falls is a three-tiered waterfall dropping more than 100 feet over volcanic cliffs. The cataract plunges onto ledges, shooting up and fanning out after each drop. An excellent vantage spot to view the falls is from a roadside pullout on the south rim of the canyon, a short distance northwest of the Lava Creek picnic area. The forested Lava Creek Trail leads to the falls on the opposite (north) side of the canyon, away from the crowds. The falls can be reached from two directions. The longer 6-mile round trip hike begins at Mammoth (Hike 2). This hike, the shorter route, begins at the Lava Creek picnic area at the head of Lava Creek Canyon near the Lava Creek Bridge. The path parallels the creek through a Douglas fir forest to an overlook at the top of the falls.

Driving directions: From Mammoth, drive 4.4 miles southeast towards Tower to the signed Lava Creek Picnic Area on the right.

From Tower Junction, drive 13.7 miles northwest towards Mammoth to the signed Lava Creek Picnic Area on the left, just after crossing the bridge over Lava Creek.

Hiking directions: Walk east across the Lava Creek highway bridge. After crossing, the unsigned trail at the east edge of the bridge heads up the hillside to the north. Cross the sage-covered plateau a short distance to a T-junction. The right fork leads 2.4 miles on the Howard Eaton Trail to the Blacktail Ponds and the Blacktail Creek trailhead. Bear left on the Lava Creek Trail, following the meadow gently downhill. A side path on the left leads to the brink of the falls in a Douglas fir forest. From here, walk along the cliff for continuous views of the cascading falls. Across the canyon is the roadside waterfall viewing area. Return along the same trail.

To hike further, the trail drops down into Lava Creek Canyon towards Mammoth (Hike 2).

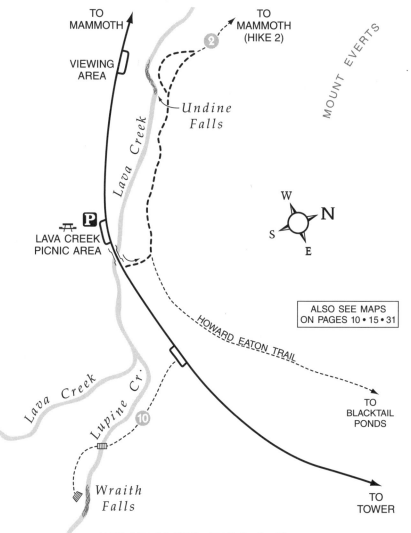

UNDINE FALLS
FROM LAVA CREEK PICNIC AREA

Hike 10
Wraith Falls

Hiking distance: 1 mile round trip
Hiking time: 30 minutes
Elevation gain: Level
Maps: U.S.G.S. Blacktail Deer Creek
Trails Illustrated Mammoth Hot Springs

Summary of hike: Wraith Falls is a beautiful 100-foot sloping cascade on an inclined rock slab in Lupine Creek, a tributary of Lava Creek. The trail is an easy, half-mile hike through an open sagebrush meadow and a mixed forest of Engelmann spruce, lodgepole pines, and Douglas fir. The trail crosses a bridge over Lupine Creek to a platform overlook of the falls.

Driving directions: From Mammoth, drive 5 miles southeast towards Tower to the Wraith Falls parking area on the right. It is located 0.4 miles past the Lava Creek picnic area.

From Tower Junction, drive 13 miles northwest towards Mammoth to the Wraith Falls parking area on the left.

Hiking directions: From the parking area, follow the well-marked trail south. The path has two short boardwalks that protect the fragile plant life in the open meadows. A small footbridge crosses over Lupine Creek. The trail ends at a wooden observation platform 100 yards in front of Wraith Falls. Return along the same trail.

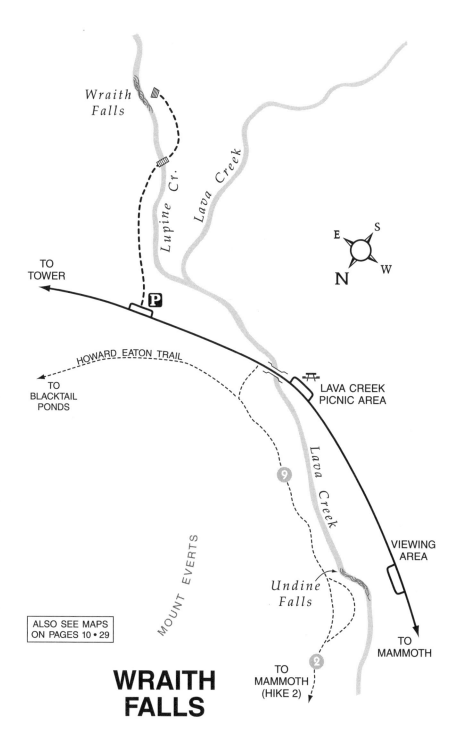

Wraith
Falls

Lupine Cr.

Lava Creek

E   S

N   W

TO
TOWER

P

HOWARD EATON TRAIL

TO
BLACKTAIL
PONDS

Lava Creek

LAVA CREEK
PICNIC AREA

9

VIEWING
AREA

MOUNT EVERTS

Undine
Falls

ALSO SEE MAPS
ON PAGES 10 • 29

TO
MAMMOTH

TO
MAMMOTH
(HIKE 2)

2

WRAITH
FALLS

Hike 11
Hellroaring Creek and
Black Canyon of the Yellowstone

Hiking distance: 4 miles round trip
Hiking time: 2 hours
Elevation gain: 700 feet
Maps: U.S.G.S. Tower Junction
Trails Illustrated Tower/Canyon

Summary of hike: Hellroaring Creek is a wide rocky creek that flows from the Absaroka-Beartooth Wilderness into the Yellowstone River. At the creek, pyramid-shaped Hellroaring Mountain lies to the north, the park's largest granite mountain, and Buffalo Plateau lies to the east. The hike crosses a suspension bridge high above the turbulent water of the Yellowstone River in the steep and narrow Black Canyon of the Yellowstone. Hellroaring Creek also offers excellent trout fishing.

Driving directions: From Tower Junction, drive 3.7 miles northwest towards Mammoth to the signed Hellroaring trailhead turnoff and turn right. Continue 0.2 miles on the unpaved road to the parking area at the road's end.
From Mammoth, drive 14.5 miles southeast towards Tower to the Hellroaring Trailhead turnoff and turn left.

Hiking directions: Head northeast across the rolling hills. Switchbacks lead down towards the Black Canyon of the Yellowstone. At 0.8 miles, a trail leading to Tower intersects from the right. Continue straight ahead to the sturdy suspension bridge crossing the surging Yellowstone River in a deep gorge. Cross the narrow bridge over the canyon, and head north through the forested draw to a junction with the Buffalo Plateau Trail at 1.5 miles. Continue north across the open sagebrush hills, reaching a pond and a trail split at two miles. The left fork circles the pond to tree-lined Hellroaring Creek. Across the creek, the Yellowstone River Trail follows the north side of the river 16 miles to Gardiner. The right fork heads upstream to a patrol cabin at just under a mile and a stock bridge shortly after. Return by retracing your route.

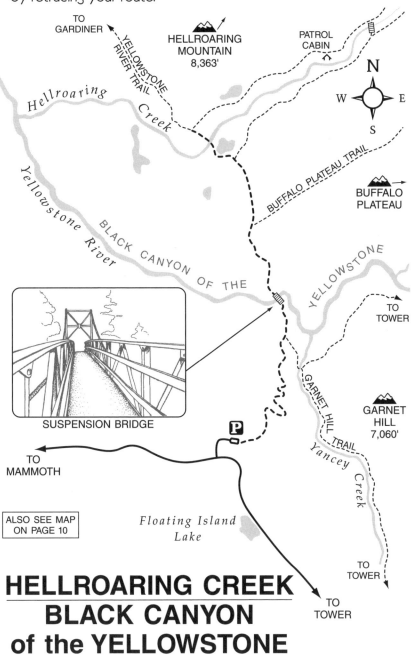

TO
GARDINER

HELLROARING MOUNTAIN 8,363'

YELLOWSTONE RIVER TRAIL

PATROL CABIN

Hellroaring Creek

N
W E
S

Yellowstone River

BLACK CANYON OF THE

BUFFALO PLATEAU TRAIL

BUFFALO PLATEAU

YELLOWSTONE

TO TOWER

SUSPENSION BRIDGE

P

GARNET HILL TRAIL

GARNET HILL 7,060'

TO
MAMMOTH

Yancey Creek

ALSO SEE MAP
ON PAGE 10

Floating Island Lake

TO TOWER

HELLROARING CREEK
BLACK CANYON
of the YELLOWSTONE

TO
TOWER

Hike 12
Lost Lake from Petrified Tree

Hiking distance: 1 mile round trip
Hiking time: 40 minutes
Elevation gain: Level
Maps: U.S.G.S. Tower Junction
Trails Illustrated Tower/Canyon

Summary of hike: Lost Lake is a six-acre mountain lake that sits in a long, tree-lined valley surrounded by steep, forested hillsides. Yellow pond lilies line the shores of the shallow, pastoral lake. This hike begins from Petrified Tree, an old redwood tree buried and entombed in ash and mud from volcanic eruptions 50 million years ago. The trail from Petrified Tree to Lost Lake follows the grassy meadows through a narrow, open valley filled with wildflowers to the head of the lake. The path continues along the north side of the lake to Roosevelt Lodge, Hike 13. (Hike 18 also includes petrified trees.)

Driving directions: From Tower Junction, drive 1.4 miles northwest towards Mammoth to the signed Petrified Tree turnoff on the left. Turn left and continue 0.5 miles on the paved road to the signed trailhead and parking area at the end of the road.

From Mammoth, drive 16.7 miles southeast towards Tower to the Petrified Tree turnoff on the right.

Hiking directions: Take the short walk up the ramp to view the fenced, 50-million-year-old petrified redwood tree. Return to the parking lot and pick up the signed trail at the end of the lot across the road. Head south into the meadow. Curve around the forested hill in the lush draw, thick with grasses and flowers. As the ravine narrows, the path follows the banks of a trickling stream. Soon the canyon opens up to a wide meadow and curves east, contouring around the hillside on the left. The trail reaches the west end of Lost Lake at a half mile. Follow the north shore of the lily pad-rimmed lake.

To hike further, the trail continues to Lost Creek Falls and Roosevelt Lodge (Hike 13). It also connects with the trail to Tower Falls (Hike 14).

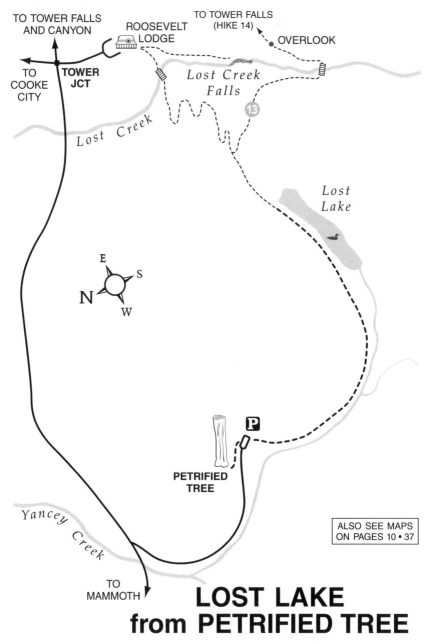

LOST LAKE
from PETRIFIED TREE

Hike 13
Lost Creek Falls and Lost Lake

Hiking distance: 4 miles round trip
Hiking time: 2 hours
Elevation gain: 450 feet
Maps: U.S.G.S. Tower Junction
       Trails Illustrated Tower/Canyon

Summary of hike: Lost Creek Falls is a 40-foot waterfall in a steep, dark-walled box canyon behind the historic Roosevelt Lodge, a log structure built in 1920 to commemorate a visit by President Theodore Roosevelt. The short path leads up the canyon through subalpine fir between moss-covered walls to the base of the falls. Back at the lodge is a connecting trail to the brink of the falls on the Lost Creek Trail. The trail leads to an overlook at the top of Lost Creek Falls. This route also connects to Lost Lake, which sits in a beautiful grassy draw filled with wildflowers. The lake is bordered on both ends by forested hills. From Lost Lake, the path continues to the ancient remains of Petrified Tree (Hike 12).

Driving directions: The trailhead is at Roosevelt Lodge, located at Tower Junction. Park on the west side of the parking lot near the lodge.

Hiking directions: From the parking area, walk to the back of Roosevelt Lodge. The trailhead is easily found directly behind the lodge. There are two trails. To begin, take the left trail 0.2 miles to a magnificent view of Lost Creek Falls from its base. This short trail is surrounded by steep canyon cliffs. Return to the trailhead and take the right fork towards Lost Lake, which immediately crosses a footbridge over Lost Creek. Continue up switchbacks through a dense Douglas fir forest to the top of the hill at 0.6 miles and a trail junction. The right trail goes to Lost Lake. First, take the left fork 0.6 miles to an overlook of Lost Creek Falls. (From here, the trail continues to Tower Falls, Hike 14.) Return 0.6 miles back to the Lost Lake trail junction. Take the west fork 0.2 miles to Lost Lake. The trail follows the north shore of the lake and continues to Petrified Tree (Hike 12). After exploring the lake, take the same trail back to Roosevelt Lodge.

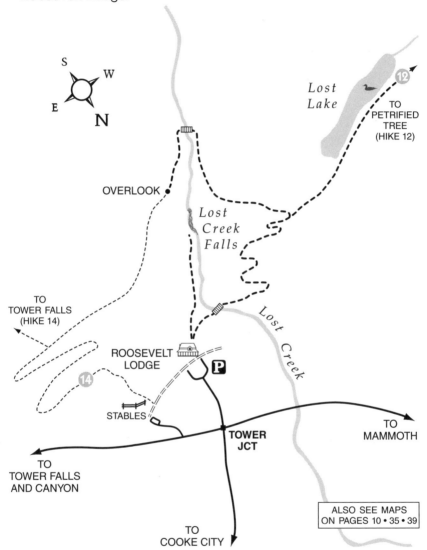

LOST CREEK FALLS
LOST LAKE

Hike 14
Roosevelt Lodge
to Tower Falls Campground

Hiking distance: 5 miles round trip
Hiking time: 2.5 hours
Elevation gain: 400 feet
Maps: U.S.G.S. Tower Junction
       Trails Illustrated Tower/Canyon

Summary of hike: This hike begins near the historic Roosevelt Lodge, a beautiful log structure built in 1920. The trail crosses large meadows and open forests to the Tower Falls Campground, across from Tower Falls. The connector trail parallels the Tower–Canyon Road, but the route is up and over a ridge, isolated in the remote backcountry. The well-defined trail is not heavily traveled and offers expansive views of the surrounding terrain.

Driving directions: From Tower Junction, drive 0.2 miles east towards Tower Falls to the Roosevelt horse stables on the right. Turn right and park in the parking area.

Hiking directions: Facing the stable information building, walk around the right side of the building. Follow the road to the forested hillside. Curve left along the base of the hill around the back side of the cabins and stables. The pack trail climbs the hill. Long, sweeping switchbacks lead up to the ridge and a signed junction at 0.6 miles. The right fork crosses Lost Creek back to Roosevelt Lodge (Hike 13) or continues to Lost Lake and Petrified Tree (Hike 12). Take the left fork across the open sage-covered meadow. Traverse the southern flank of the forested draw to a ridge at an aspen grove. Wind through open, forests and cross the rolling, flowering meadows dotted with trees. The views extend from The Narrows of the Yellowstone River and across the Lamar Valley to The Thunderer. At 2.5 miles, short, steep switchbacks quickly descend the hillside to Tower Creek. Cross the wooden bridge over the creek to a junction. The left fork leads to the Hamilton Store and Tower Falls (Hike 16). Take the right fork 0.2 miles to a signed junction, following the cascading creek upstream past wild roses and raspberry bushes. The right fork follows Tower Creek (Hike 15). The left fork leads up along a railing to the campground.

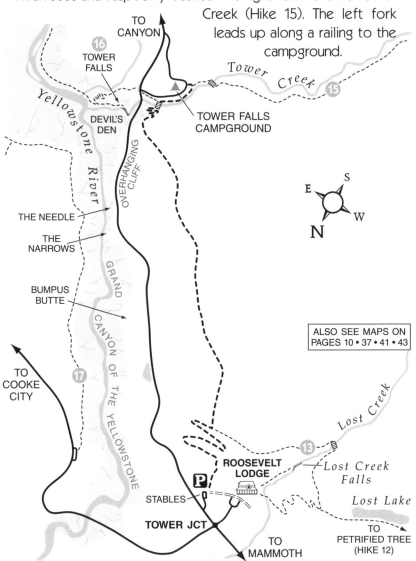

ROOSEVELT LODGE to TOWER FALLS CAMPGROUND

Hike 15
Tower Creek Trail

Hiking distance: 8 miles round trip to Carnelian Creek
(easy creekside stroll is variable)
Hiking time: 1—5 hours
Elevation gain: 400 feet
Maps: U.S.G.S. Tower Junction and Mount Washburn
Trails Illustrated Tower/Canyon

Summary of hike: Tower Creek begins on the north flank of the Washburn Range and joins the Yellowstone River just downstream from the 132-foot Tower Falls (Hike 16). The Tower Creek Trail begins at the Tower Falls Campground in a forest of Douglas fir and Engelmann spruce. The trail parallels the north side of the creek up Tower Creek Canyon. The area, burned in the 1988 Yellowstone fires, is an interesting study of the effects of the fire. Notice how the fallen trees have altered the course of the creek and created new pools and eddies. The trail can be shortened to an easy, meandering creekside stroll of any length.

Driving directions: The Tower Falls Campground is 2.4 miles south of Tower Junction and 16.5 miles north of Canyon. The campground is directly across the road from the Hamilton Store and the Tower Falls trailhead. Turn west and drive 0.3 miles towards the campground. Park on the left, just before the employee service road.

Hiking directions: Walk twenty yards back down the campground entrance road to the signed trail on the left. Descend into a forest of fir and spruce to a signed junction. The right fork leads to Roosevelt Lodge (Hike 14). Bear left on the Tower Creek Trail along the south bank of the creek. Take the left fork by the sign-in register, and follow the cascading creek to a footbridge. Cross the old wooden bridge over Tower Creek. The trail continues southwest through the burn area. Cross the meadow, teaming with wildflowers and numerous

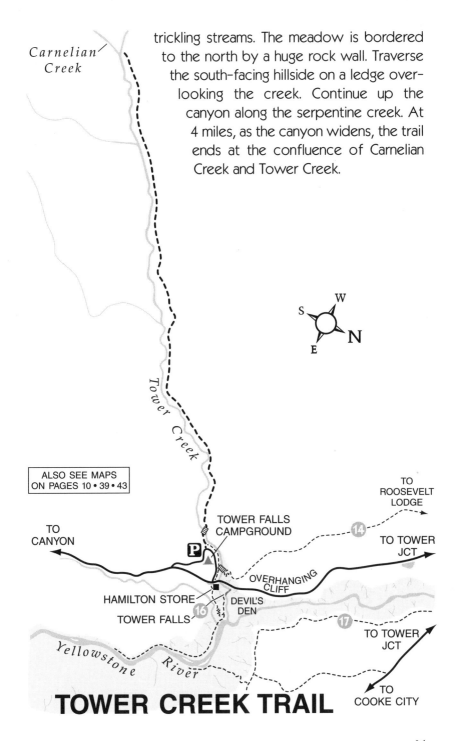

trickling streams. The meadow is bordered to the north by a huge rock wall. Traverse the south-facing hillside on a ledge overlooking the creek. Continue up the canyon along the serpentine creek. At 4 miles, as the canyon widens, the trail ends at the confluence of Carnelian Creek and Tower Creek.

Carnelian Creek

Tower Creek

ALSO SEE MAPS
ON PAGES 10 • 39 • 43

TO ROOSEVELT LODGE

TO CANYON

TOWER FALLS CAMPGROUND

P

14

TO TOWER JCT

OVERHANGING CLIFF

HAMILTON STORE

DEVIL'S DEN

TOWER FALLS

16

17

TO TOWER JCT

Yellowstone River

TO COOKE CITY

TOWER CREEK TRAIL

Hike 16
Tower Falls and the
Yellowstone River Trail

Hiking distance: 3 miles round trip
Hiking time: 2 hours
Elevation gain: 300 feet
Maps: U.S.G.S. Tower Junction
       Trails Illustrated Tower/Canyon

Summary of hike: Tower Falls is a 132-foot cataract on Tower Creek, surrounded by majestic, volcanic spires that rise sixty feet above the falls. The waterfall is adjacent to the Yellowstone River in the Grand Canyon of the Yellowstone. The trail descends the 200-foot cliffs into the river canyon where Tower Creek joins the river. The trail passes two distinct viewpoints of Tower Falls. The first view is part way down the cliffs at a magnificent overlook of the plunging waterfall and eroded minarets. The second view is in the creek-carved gorge at the base of the thunderous falls. At the Yellowstone River, the path continues between the steep walls of the Grand Canyon.

Driving directions: The Tower Falls parking lot is 2.4 miles south of Tower Junction and 16.5 miles north of Canyon. There is a Hamilton Store on the east side of the road near the parking lot.

Hiking directions: From the parking lot, walk towards the Hamilton Store. The trailhead is clearly visible along the right side of the store. A short distance from here is the first overlook of Tower Falls. Continue down into the canyon, winding through spruce and Douglas fir to a trail junction. Take the left fork and follow Tower Creek upstream to the base of the falls. It is here that a man was heard to exclaim, "This is the place to see it from, Phyllis!"

After viewing the falls, return to the junction. Now take the left (east) fork downhill to the Yellowstone River. Continue up river to the right on a gravel bar. The trail continues beneath the ragged walls of the Grand Canyon of the Yellowstone. The open area along this portion of the canyon encourages off-trail exploring. Return on the same trail back to the Tower Falls parking lot.

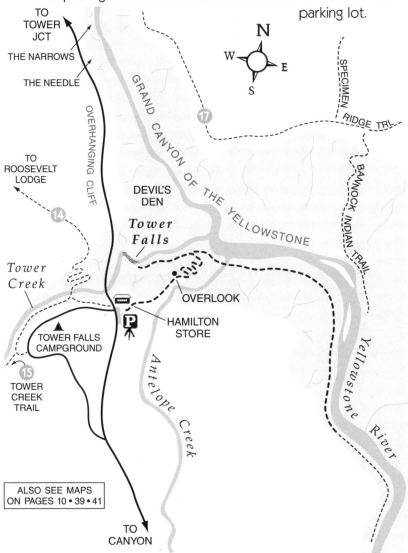

TOWER FALLS
YELLOWSTONE RIVER TRAIL
GRAND CANYON of the YELLOWSTONE

Hike 17
Yellowstone River Picnic Area Trail

Hiking distance: 4 miles round trip or 3.7 mile loop
Hiking time: 2 hours
Elevation gain: 300 feet
Maps: U.S.G.S. Tower Junction
Trails Illustrated Tower/Canyon

Summary of hike: This easy hike parallels the northern end of the Grand Canyon of the Yellowstone and the Yellowstone River along the edge of the canyon rim. From 700 feet above the river, the hike offers continuous views of vertical basalt columns and eroded rock formations, including The Narrows (the narrowest section of the 23-mile-long canyon), Bumpus Butte, The Needle, Overhanging Cliff, Devil's Den, and the towers at Tower Falls.

Driving directions: From Tower Junction, drive 1.2 miles on the Northeast Entrance Road towards Cooke City to the Yellowstone River Picnic Area on the right.

Hiking directions: The signed trail begins on the east side of the picnic area. Head south, gaining 200 feet up the grassy hillside to the ridge. From the ridge are views across the canyon and down to the Yellowstone River. From here, the trail levels out and continues southeast along the ridge. At 1.5 miles, the canyon and trail curve left. The trail crosses the plateau and connects with the Specimen Ridge Trail and the Bannock Indian Trail, which drops south into the canyon and down to the river. This junction is the turnaround point. Return to the trailhead along the same trail.

For a 3.7-mile loop hike, at the junction with the Specimen Ridge Trail, take the downhill route to the north. Wind through aspen and Douglas fir groves and grassland meadows to the Northeast Entrance Road at just over one mile. Follow the road to the left for 0.7 miles, returning to the trailhead.

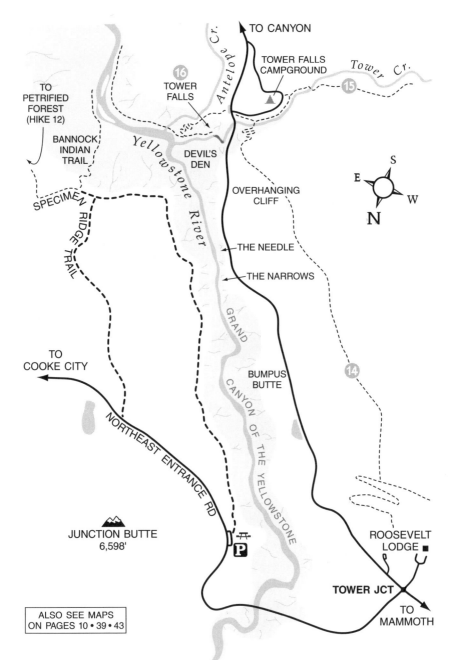

TO CANYON

TOWER FALLS CAMPGROUND

Tower Cr.

Antelope Cr.

16 TOWER FALLS

15

TO PETRIFIED FOREST (HIKE 12)

BANNOCK INDIAN TRAIL

Yellowstone River

DEVIL'S DEN

OVERHANGING CLIFF

S

E —⊛— W

N

SPECIMEN RIDGE TRAIL

THE NEEDLE

THE NARROWS

TO COOKE CITY

GRAND CANYON OF THE YELLOWSTONE

BUMPUS BUTTE

14

NORTHEAST ENTRANCE RD

JUNCTION BUTTE 6,598'

P 🏕

ROOSEVELT LODGE ■

TOWER JCT

TO MAMMOTH

ALSO SEE MAPS ON PAGES 10 • 39 • 43

YELLOWSTONE RIVER
PICNIC AREA TRAIL

Hike 18
Petrified Forest

Hiking distance: 3.5 miles round trip
Hiking time: 2 hours
Elevation gain: 1,600 feet
Maps: U.S.G.S. Lamar Canyon
Trails Illustrated Tower/Canyon

Summary of hike: The Petrified Forest on Specimen Ridge, extending over 40 square miles, contains one of the most extensive petrified forests in the world. Lava flows engulfed and entombed the deciduous forest 50 million years ago, preserving the still-standing ancient remains. Among the specimens are redwoods, sycamores, oaks, and maples. This hike is the shortest route to the Petrified Forest and is brutally steep. The trail climbs nearly straight up the ridge with little finesse. The impressive fossilized forest and panoramic vistas are worth every step of the steep ascent.

Driving directions: From Tower Junction, drive 5 miles on the Northeast Entrance Road towards Cooke City. The signed trailhead turnout is on the left.

From the Slough Creek Campground turnoff, drive 0.8 miles southwest to the signed trailhead turnout.

Hiking directions: Follow the old faint road south for a hundred yards, and bear right on the distinct footpath. Cross the flat grass and sage meadow to the base of the mountain. Begin the ascent of the mountain, reaching a Douglas fir grove at one mile. Follow the ridge, curving to the right around the north flank of the mountain. Pass a larger stand of Douglas fir and continue steeply uphill, reaching a trail split near the top. Begin the loop to the right, following the north side of the ridge. Just after emerging from the forest is a petrified tree stump on the right side of the trail. Another stump is embedded in the path. Traverse the narrow cliff-hugging path past numerous massive stumps to a sloping meadow. Curve left, making the final ascent up the grassy hillside to the ridge and the Specimen Ridge Trail. Bear left and follow the ridge to the knoll. Mount Washburn rises in the south, and the Lamar Valley lies to the north. Side paths lead to the numerous petrified stumps. Leave the knoll and descend on the rocky path past many more fossilized trees, completing the loop at the treeline. Take the right fork and retrace your route.

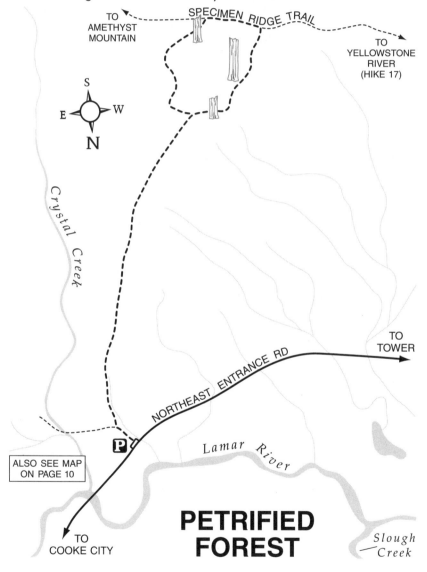

Hike 19
Slough Creek

Hiking distance: 2 miles round trip (or further)
Hiking time: 1 hour
Elevation gain: 400 feet
Maps: U.S.G.S. Lamar Canyon
            Trails Illustrated Tower/Canyon

Summary of hike: Slough Creek is a slow-rolling, meandering creek in a gorgeous glacial valley. The creek is a popular fishing destination, well known for its cutthroat trout. The hike begins near the secluded Slough Creek Campground at the mouth of the canyon and follows a historic wagon road through open fir and aspen forests. The road is still used by horse-drawn wagons for access to the Silver Tip Ranch, located just outside the park. The trail emerges in the broad open valley at an oxbow bend in Slough Creek. Beyond the crescent-shaped bend, the creek snakes through scenic, wildflower-laden meadows surrounded by mountains.

Driving directions: From Tower Junction, drive 5.8 miles on the Northeast Entrance Road towards Cooke City. Turn left at the signed Slough Creek Campground turnoff, and drive 1.8 miles to the signed trailhead parking area on the right.

From the northeast entrance to Yellowstone National Park, drive 22.2 miles southwest to the signed Slough Creek Campground turnoff on the right.

Hiking directions: Head east on the old wagon road past the trailhead sign. Wind up the open forest past large glacial boulders, reaching a small saddle covered with flowers at a half mile. Curve right, looping around the large rock formation as the trail levels out. Begin the gradual descent through the forest, and emerge in the gorgeous meadow at the banks of Slough Creek, backed by a large granite wall. A short distance ahead is a signed junction with the Buffalo Plateau Trail on the left. This is the turnaround spot for a 2-mile round-trip hike.

To hike further, the Buffalo Plateau Trail crosses the creek and meadow, climbing north up to Buffalo Plateau. The Slough Creek Trail continues east up the valley, crossing a ridge to the second meadow. An enjoyable third option is to follow the angler trails through the meadow along the banks of the tranquil, meandering creek. The area is so beautiful and vast, any route will be memorable.

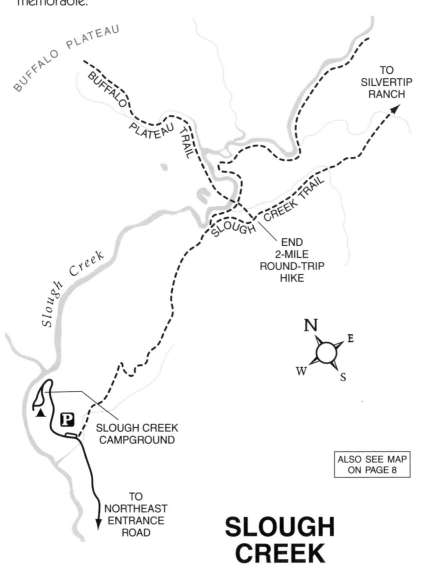

BUFFALO PLATEAU

BUFFALO PLATEAU TRAIL

TO SILVERTIP RANCH

SLOUGH CREEK TRAIL

Slough Creek

END 2-MILE ROUND-TRIP HIKE

N
E
W
S

SLOUGH CREEK CAMPGROUND

ALSO SEE MAP ON PAGE 8

TO NORTHEAST ENTRANCE ROAD

SLOUGH CREEK

Hike 20
Trout Lake

Hiking distance: 2.2 miles round trip
Hiking time: 1 hour
Elevation gain: 200 feet
Maps: U.S.G.S. Abiathar Peak and Mount Hornaday
      Trails Illustrated Tower/Canyon

Summary of hike: Trout Lake, a great rainbow trout fishing lake, sits in a beautiful bowl at the base of Mount Hornaday. The round, twelve-acre lake is surrounded by rolling meadows, evergreen forests, and a sheer rock mountain wall to the north. From the scenic lake are views of Mount Hornaday, The Thunderer, Druid Peak, and Frederick Peak.

Driving directions: From Tower Junction, drive 17.8 miles on the Northeast Entrance Road towards Cooke City to the unmarked trailhead pullout on the left. The pullout is 1.2 miles southwest of the Pebble Creek Campground.

From the northeast entrance to Yellowstone National Park, drive 10.4 miles southwest to the unmarked pullout.

Hiking directions: From the parking pullout, hike west past the trail sign towards the Engelmann spruce and Douglas fir forest. Begin ascending the hillside to the forested ridge. Along the way, the cascading outlet stream of Trout Lake tumbles down the drainage to the left of the trail. At 0.6 miles, the trail reaches the southeast end of Trout Lake at its outlet. Cross the log bridge over the creek. Once across, the trail follows the forested shoreline. A short distance ahead, the trail leaves the forest and emerges into open, rolling meadows with a wide variety of wildflowers. Continue along the shoreline, crossing a small bridge over the lake's inlet stream. Circle the perimeter of the lake back to the junction by the outlet stream, completing the loop.

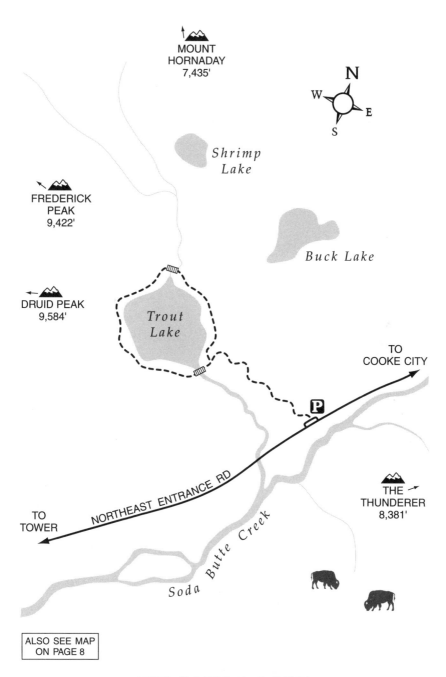

MOUNT
HORNADAY
7,435'

N
W E
S

*Shrimp
Lake*

FREDERICK
PEAK
9,422'

Buck Lake

DRUID PEAK
9,584'

*Trout
Lake*

TO
COOKE CITY

P

THE
THUNDERER
8,381'

TO
TOWER

NORTHEAST ENTRANCE RD

Soda Butte Creek

ALSO SEE MAP
ON PAGE 8

TROUT LAKE

Hike 21
Pebble Creek Trail
from Pebble Creek Campground

Hiking distance: 5—7 miles round trip (or 12-mile shuttle)
Hiking time: 3—4 hours
Elevation gain: 1,200 feet
Maps: U.S.G.S. Abiathar Peak
  Trails Illustrated Tower/Canyon

Summary of hike: The Pebble Creek Trail is a 12-mile trail with trailheads at the Pebble Creek Campground and the Warm Creek picnic area. This hike begins at the Pebble Creek Campground. The forested trail, interspersed with small meadows, steadily climbs between 10,000-foot mountain peaks. This trail may be combined with Hike 22 for a 12-mile shuttle hike. For the one-way hike, it is recommended to begin from the Warm Creek Trailhead (Hike 22), which gains the majority of the elevation in the first 1.5 miles.

Driving directions: From Tower Junction, drive 18.8 miles on the Northeast Entrance Road towards Cooke City. Turn left at the signed Pebble Creek Campground turnoff. Park in the day-use parking spaces 0.2 miles ahead on the left.

From the northeast entrance to Yellowstone National Park, drive 9.2 miles southwest to the signed Pebble Creek Campground turnoff on the right.

Hiking directions: Walk towards Pebble Creek, crossing the wooden footbridge over the creek next to campsite 32 and the restrooms. Head through the small meadow and ascend the hillside. The Pebble Creek Trail from the Northeast Entrance Road merges with the campground trail on a knoll at 0.2 miles. Bear left and climb another short hill to a view of Barronette Peak's southern flank. Cross the level area to the base of the mountain. Begin the ascent up the steep canyon, staying above the creek to the east. Switchbacks lead to a small meadow at one mile with great views of The Thunderer to the southeast.

This is a good turnaround spot for a short hike.

To hike further, continue through the lodgepole pine, spruce, and Douglas fir forest, crossing several tributary streams to the first crossing of Pebble Creek at 3.5 miles. Elevation gain continues gradually but steadily until reaching the Upper Meadows (Hike 22) and the Warm Creek trailhead, 7.5 miles further.

TO
HIKE 22
TRAILHEAD

BARRONETTE
PEAK
10,442'

CUTOFF

END
HIKE 22

HIKE 22

MONTANA
WYOMING

NORTHEAST
ENTRANCE

END
HIKE 21

BARRONETTE

ABIATHAR

NE ENTRANCE RD

MOUNT
HORNADAY
10,036'

HORNADAY

Yellowstone
National Park

HIKE 21

PEBBLE CREEK TRAIL
HIKES 21 AND 22

Pebble Creek

TO
COOKE CITY

N
W   E
S

PEBBLE CREEK
CAMPGROUND

NE ENTRANCE RD

Soda Butte Creek

P

ALSO SEE MAPS
ON PAGES 8 • 55

TO
TOWER

**PEBBLE
CREEK TRAIL**
FROM
CAMPGROUND

Hike 22
Pebble Creek Trail from Warm Creek

Hiking distance: 7 miles round trip (or 12-mile shuttle)
Hiking time: 4 hours
Elevation gain: 800 feet
Maps: U.S.G.S. Cutoff Mountain
       Trails Illustrated Tower/Canyon

Summary of hike: The Pebble Creek Trail is a 12-mile trail with trailheads at Warm Creek and the Pebble Creek Campground (Hike 21). This hike begins at Warm Creek and climbs to the Upper Meadows in a glacial valley at the north end of Barronette Peak. From the wildflower-covered meadow are panoramic views of the Absaroka Range and many of its peaks. The trail parallels Pebble Creek through the scenic valley for miles before reentering the forest. This trail may be combined with Hike 21 for a 12-mile shuttle hike.

Driving directions: From Tower Junction, drive 26.8 miles on the Northeast Entrance Road towards Cooke City. Turn left at the signed Warm Creek Trailhead turnoff and park in the lot 0.1 miles ahead. (The turnoff is 8 miles beyond the Pebble Creek Campground.)
    From the northeast entrance to Yellowstone National Park, drive 1.2 miles southwest to the signed Warm Creek Trailhead turnoff on the right.

Hiking directions: Follow the signed trail north, heading steadily uphill through the lush spruce and fir forest. At 0.4 miles, the trail bears left (west) on a more gradual slope. Continue climbing up the mountain. Near the top, emerge from the forest. Cross a talus slope with views of the Soda Butte Creek valley and the surrounding glacial peaks. Reenter the forest for the final ascent to the 8,200-foot saddle, the high point of the hike at 1.5 miles. Gradually descend 200 feet to the high mountain meadow and Pebble Creek. Carefully ford the creek and head downstream through the expansive meadow dotted with spruce and fir trees. The trail continues 1.8 miles west through the Upper Meadows past numerous trickling streams and vistas of the surrounding peaks. At 3.5 miles, the trail reaches a second creek crossing near the west end of the meadow. This is the turnaround spot.

To hike further, the trail stays level for several miles before descending 1,000 feet to the Pebble Creek Campground, 8.5 miles ahead (Hike 21).

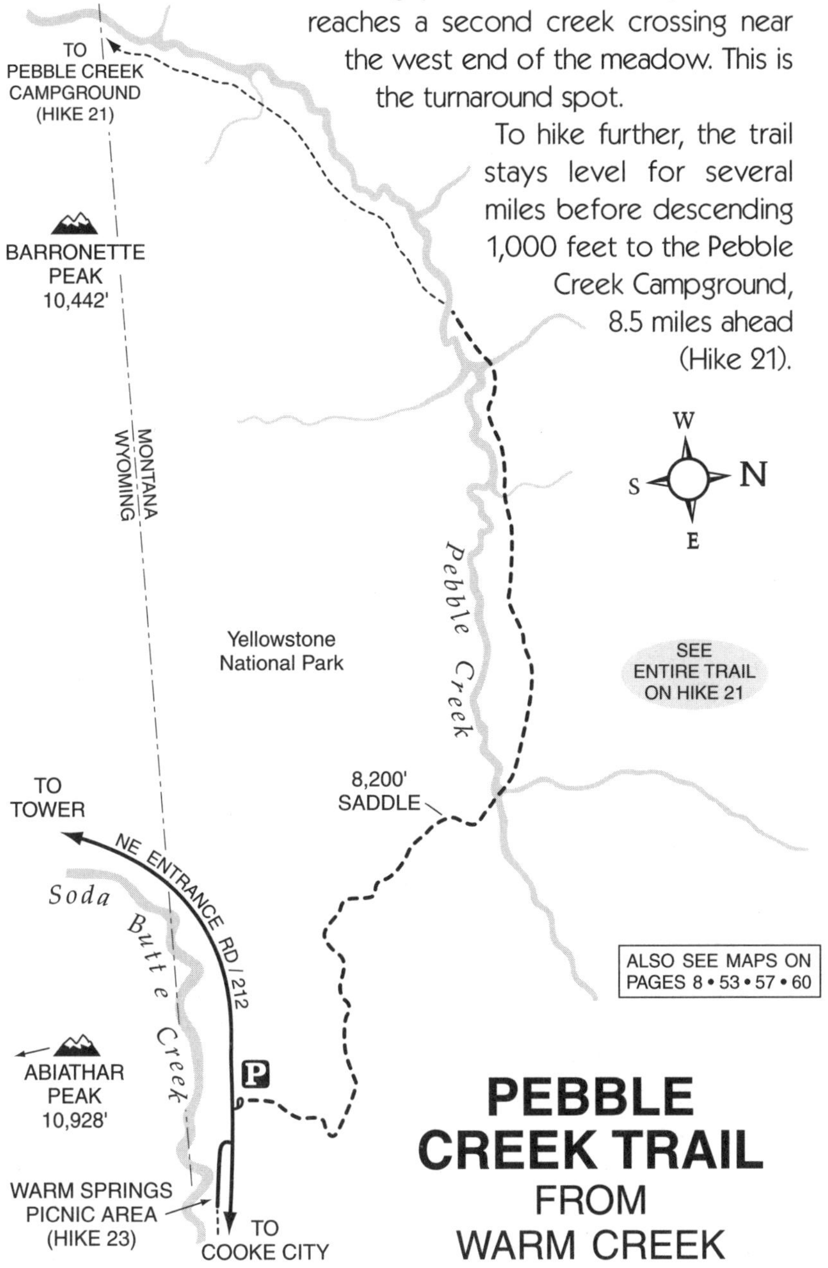

TO
PEBBLE CREEK
CAMPGROUND
(HIKE 21)

BARRONETTE
PEAK
10,442'

MONTANA
WYOMING

Yellowstone
National Park

Pebble Creek

W
S ←⊕→ N
E

SEE
ENTIRE TRAIL
ON HIKE 21

TO
TOWER

8,200'
SADDLE

NE ENTRANCE RD / 212

Soda

Butte Creek

ALSO SEE MAPS ON
PAGES 8 • 53 • 57 • 60

ABIATHAR
PEAK
10,928'

P

WARM SPRINGS
PICNIC AREA
(HIKE 23)

TO
COOKE CITY

PEBBLE CREEK TRAIL
FROM
WARM CREEK

Hike 23
Bannock Trail

Hiking distance: 4.8 miles round trip
Hiking time: 2.5 hours
Elevation gain: 130 feet
Maps: U.S.G.S. Cooke City and Cutoff Mountain
       Trails Illustrated Tower/Canyon

Summary of hike: The Bannock Trail is a short portion of the Bannock Indian route used to reach bison hunting grounds. The trail begins at Silver Gate in the North Absaroka Wilderness. The near-level terrain parallels Soda Butte Creek, a major tributary of the Lamar River, into Yellowstone National Park. The trail crosses several streams through open meadows and forest groves.

Driving directions: From the northeast entrance station of Yellowstone National Park, drive 1.1 miles outside the park to Monument Avenue in Silver Gate. Turn right and drive 0.2 miles, crossing over Soda Butte Creek, to the end of the road. Turn right on Bannock Trail and continue 0.1 miles to the end of the road at the signed trailhead. Park in pullouts alongside the road.
    From downtown Silver Gate, turn south from Highway 212 onto Monument Avenue. Follow the directions above.

Hiking directions: Head west past the trailhead sign along the base of Amphitheater Mountain. The trail skirts the south edge of the meadow under the shadow of Abiathar Peak and Barronette Peak. Past the meadow, meander through a lush lodgepole forest. Ford a wide tributary stream of Soda Butte Creek and continue west. (Downfall logs can be used to cross the stream 20 yards downstream.) Across the canyon are the bald peaks of Miller Mountain and Meridian Peak. At one mile a sign along the trail marks the boundary between the Shoshone National Forest and Yellowstone National Park. Weave through the quiet forest, reaching the banks of Soda Butte Creek at 2 miles. Follow the creekside ledge downstream to a clearing by a feeder stream. Across Soda Butte Creek is the Warm Creek picnic area. To access the picnic area, you must wade across the creek. To return, take the same trail back.

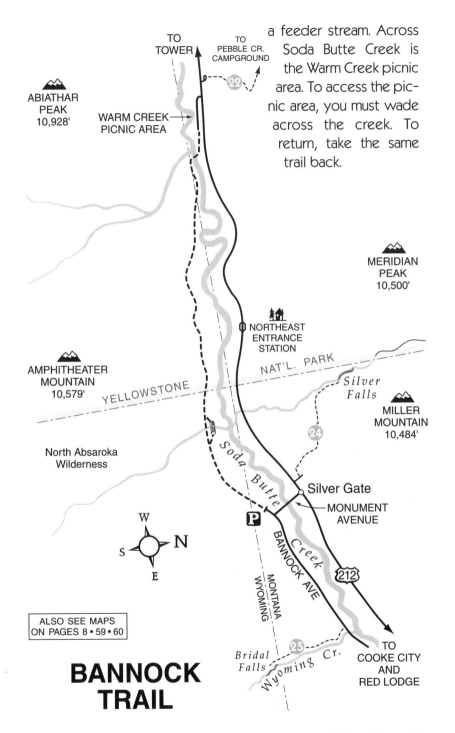

TO TOWER

TO PEBBLE CR. CAMPGROUND

22

ABIATHAR PEAK 10,928'

WARM CREEK PICNIC AREA

MERIDIAN PEAK 10,500'

NORTHEAST ENTRANCE STATION

AMPHITHEATER MOUNTAIN 10,579'

YELLOWSTONE

NAT'L. PARK

Silver Falls

MILLER MOUNTAIN 10,484'

North Absaroka Wilderness

Soda Butte

24

Creek

Silver Gate

MONUMENT AVENUE

P

W

N

S

E

BANNOCK AVE

MONTANA WYOMING

212

ALSO SEE MAPS ON PAGES 8 • 59 • 60

Bridal Falls

25

Wyoming Cr.

TO COOKE CITY AND RED LODGE

BANNOCK TRAIL

Hike 24
Silver Falls

Hiking distance: 2 miles round trip
Hiking time: 1 hour
Elevation gain: 350 feet
Maps: U.S.G.S. Cooke City and Cutoff Mountain
      Trail Illustrated Tower/Canyon

Summary of hike: Silver Falls is a long and narrow waterfall that drops more than 100 feet over a limestone cliff. The hike to the falls is along the eastern border of Yellowstone National Park, beginning from the town of Silver Gate. The last section of the trail parallels Silver Creek to the base of this beautiful falls.

Driving directions: From the northeast entrance station of Yellowstone National Park, drive 1 mile outside the park to the west edge of Silver Gate and park.

Hiking directions: Walk 0.1 mile west on Highway 212 towards Yellowstone National Park. Take the unpaved road on the right 30 yards uphill to the powerlines and private road sign. Take the trail on the left, following the powerpoles 20 yards to the trail arrow sign on the right. Bear right on the footpath through the dense forest to an unsigned three-way trail split. Take the middle fork, straight ahead, to an old grass-covered road and another trail arrow. Bear left on the road. A short distance ahead, the road curves right to another road at a T-junction. Follow the arrow sign to the left through the burn area, reaching the east bank of Silver Creek. Take the creekside trail upstream above the drainage. As you near the head of the canyon, the trail becomes rocky. Descend into the canyon to the trail's end at the base of Silver Falls. Return along the same path.

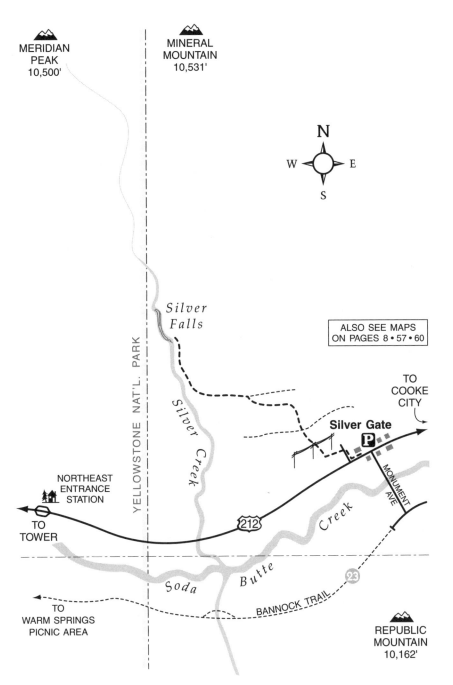

MERIDIAN
PEAK
10,500'

MINERAL
MOUNTAIN
10,531'

N
W   E
S

*Silver
Falls*

ALSO SEE MAPS
ON PAGES 8 • 57 • 60

TO
COOKE
CITY

Silver Gate

P

Silver Creek

YELLOWSTONE NAT'L. PARK

NORTHEAST
ENTRANCE
STATION

MONUMENT AVE.

TO
TOWER

US 212

Creek

23

Soda   *Butte*

BANNOCK TRAIL

TO
WARM SPRINGS
PICNIC AREA

REPUBLIC
MOUNTAIN
10,162'

SILVER FALLS

Hike 25
Bridal Falls

Hiking distance: 0.6 miles round trip
Hiking time: 15 minutes
Elevation gain: 50 feet
Maps: U.S.G.S. Cooke City
       Rocky Mountain Survey—Cooke City

Summary of hike: Bridal Falls (unofficially named) drops out of steep granite cliffs to a ledge. From the ledge, the water shoots out horizontally, dropping more than forty additional feet into a misty pool. Ferns and moss grow along these sheer rock walls. The trail is a short and easy path that parallels Wyoming Creek through the forest.

Driving directions: From the northeast entrance of Yellowstone National Park, drive 1.2 miles east (outside the park) to Monument Avenue in Silver Gate. Turn right and drive 0.2 miles to the end of the road. Turn left on Bannock Avenue, and continue 0.8 miles to the Wyoming Creek bridge, the only bridge along the road. Park off the road before crossing the bridge.

Hiking directions: From the road, walk upstream along the west side of Wyoming Creek. The path leads south for 0.3 miles to the base of the falls and pool. The mountain on the left (east) of the falls is Republic Mountain. To the right (west) is Wall Rock. Return along the same trail.

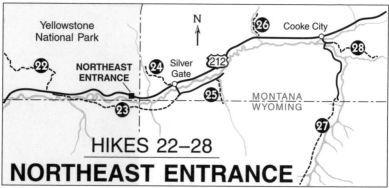

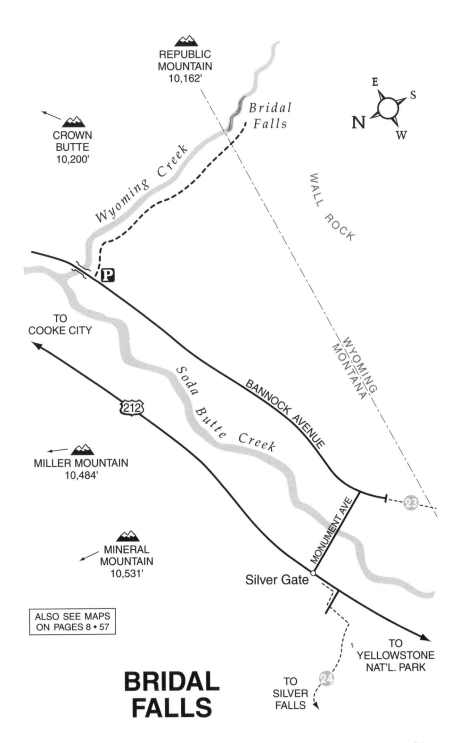

REPUBLIC
MOUNTAIN
10,162'

*Bridal
Falls*

E
N   S
W

CROWN
BUTTE
10,200'

Wyoming Creek

WALL ROCK

P

TO
COOKE CITY

WYOMING
MONTANA

Soda Butte Creek

BANNOCK AVENUE

212

MILLER MOUNTAIN
10,484'

MINERAL
MOUNTAIN
10,531'

MONUMENT AVE

23

ALSO SEE MAPS
ON PAGES 8 • 57

Silver Gate

TO
YELLOWSTONE
NAT'L. PARK

TO
SILVER
FALLS

24

BRIDAL
FALLS

Hike 26
Sheep Creek Falls

Hiking distance: 0.6 miles round trip
Hiking time: .5 hours
Elevation gain: 200 feet
Maps: U.S.G.S. Cooke City
       Rocky Mountain Survey—Cooke City

Summary of hike: Sheep Creek Falls is a magnificent, full-bodied waterfall surrounded by mountain peaks. Although it is only 0.3 miles to the falls, it is not an easy hike. It is a scramble up canyon and over timber along Sheep Creek. There is not a defined trail, and it is not recommended for youngsters. The hike climbs through a burn area from the 1988 Yellowstone fires.

Driving directions: From the northeast entrance station of Yellowstone National Park, drive 2.8 miles east (outside the park) to the parking pullout on the right side of the highway and on the west side of the Sheep Creek bridge. The trailhead is located 1.6 miles east of Silver Gate and 1.1 miles west of Cooke City.

Hiking directions: From the parking pullout, cross to the north side of Highway 212. Walk upstream along the east side of Sheep Creek. The trail fades in and out. Scramble upstream, using Sheep Creek as your guide. After climbing over and around down trees for a quarter mile, the canyon curves to the right. From this spot, the magnificence of Sheep Creek Falls is directly in view. Return by heading back downstream to the highway.

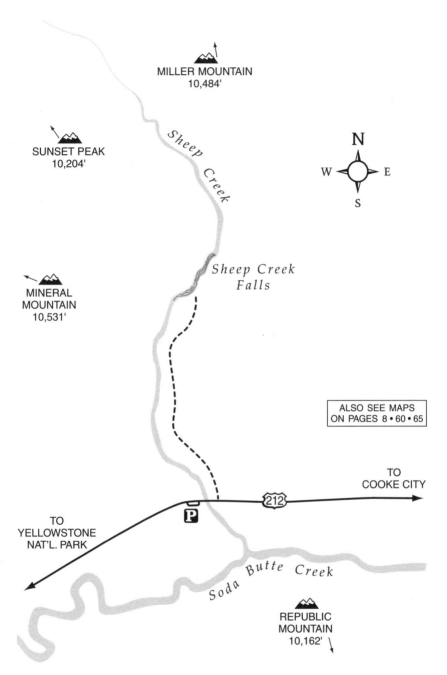

MILLER MOUNTAIN
10,484'

SUNSET PEAK
10,204'

Sheep Creek

N
W   E
S

MINERAL
MOUNTAIN
10,531'

Sheep Creek
Falls

ALSO SEE MAPS
ON PAGES 8 • 60 • 65

TO
COOKE CITY

212

P

TO
YELLOWSTONE
NAT'L. PARK

Soda Butte Creek

REPUBLIC
MOUNTAIN
10,162'

SHEEP CREEK FALLS

Hike 27
Republic Creek Trail

Hiking distance: 5.6 miles round trip
Hiking time: 3 hours
Elevation gain: 450 feet
Maps: U.S.G.S. Cooke City and Pilot Peak
       Trails Illustrated Tower/Canyon

Summary of hike: The Republic Creek Trail begins at Cooke City and follows a high mountain meadow parallel to Republic Creek. The trail crosses over Republic Pass at 4.5 miles, just west of Republic Peak, and connects with the Cache Creek Trail to the Lamar Valley in Yellowstone Park. This hike follows the first portion of the trail through the creek valley to the headwall at the north face of Republic Peak. There are scenic vistas of the surrounding peaks and a beautiful display of wildflowers.

Driving directions: From the northeast entrance station of Yellowstone National Park, drive 3.8 miles outside the park to Cooke City and Republic Road on the right. Turn right one block to a road split. Take the right fork on the unpaved road, and head past some homes. Curve left, heading up the narrow mountain road, and drive 1.3 miles to the signed Republic Creek Trail on the right. The trailhead is just past some old cabins and remnants of the mine. Park in one of the small pullouts.

From downtown Cooke City, turn south from Highway 212 onto Republic Road. Follow the directions above.

Hiking directions: Head to the south on the signed footpath, crossing a small feeder stream of Republic Creek. At a quarter mile, the trail levels out and leads through the dense forest with a lush understory of grasses and flowers. Cross a rocky streambed, and emerge in an expansive rolling meadow dotted with trees and teaming with flowers. Continue south up the alpine valley between mountain peaks. At 1.5 miles the trail reaches Republic Meadow. This is a good turnaround spot for a 3-mile hike.

To continue hiking, skirt the west edge of the meadow, crossing several streams to the head of the valley at 2.8 miles. The area sits in an ice-scoured cirque of mountains at the base of Republic Peak and Republic Pass. From the bowl, the trail steeply ascends the mountain to Republic Pass and Yellowstone Park at 4.5 miles.

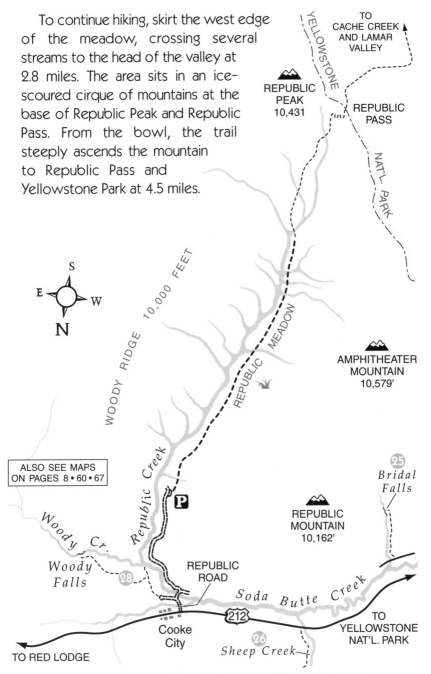

REPUBLIC CREEK TRAIL

Hike 28
Woody Falls

Hiking distance: 3 miles round trip
Hiking time: 2 hours
Elevation gain: 700 feet
Maps: U.S.G.S. Cooke City
      Rocky Mountain Survey—Cooke City

Summary of hike: Woody Falls is a spectacular 150-foot, three-tiered waterfall with a pool at the base. The falls is a popular destination for the locals as well as a cross-country ski trail in the winter. The trailhead is located in downtown Cooke City. The hike begins on an old mining road that leads to the Mohawk Mine.

Driving directions: From the northeast entrance station of Yellowstone National Park, drive 3.8 miles outside the park to Republic Road on the right in Cooke City. Turn right one block to a road split. Take the left fork on the unpaved road, and drive 0.2 miles to the loop at the end of the road. Park on the side of the road.

    If you do not mind fording a stream and prefer to walk from downtown Cooke City, a second trailhead is located at the south end of River Street behind the general store. At the end of River Street is a buck fence and trail entrance. Walk south on the trail past old log cabins. Wade across Soda Butte Creek to the parking area.

Hiking directions: From the parking area off of Republic Road, walk up the jeep road to the southeast. Within five minutes from the trailhead is a well-defined footpath on the left. This is the trail to Woody Falls. For a short side trip, stay on the jeep road an additional 200 yards, just past a sign reading "Woody Creek Ski Trail." Take the spur trail to the right 100 yards to a beautiful cascade and smaller waterfall. Return to the main jeep trail and the Woody Falls Trail. The well-worn footpath begins a steady uphill climb through the forest. As the canyon below narrows, the falls can be heard on the right. Spur trails lead to the canyon edge for a variety of commanding overviews of Woody Falls. Return along the same trail.

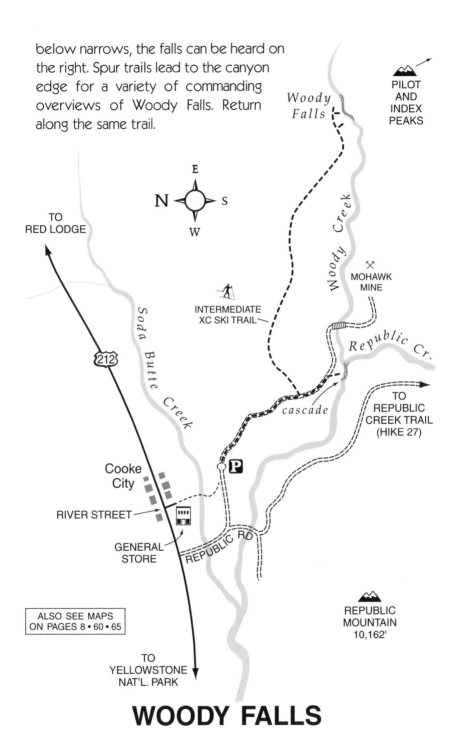

PILOT AND INDEX PEAKS

Woody Falls

Woody Creek

E

N ☼ S

W

TO RED LODGE

MOHAWK MINE

INTERMEDIATE XC SKI TRAIL

Soda Butte Creek

212

Republic Cr.

cascade

TO REPUBLIC CREEK TRAIL (HIKE 27)

P

Cooke City

RIVER STREET

GENERAL STORE

REPUBLIC RD

REPUBLIC MOUNTAIN 10,162'

ALSO SEE MAPS ON PAGES 8 • 60 • 65

TO YELLOWSTONE NAT'L. PARK

WOODY FALLS

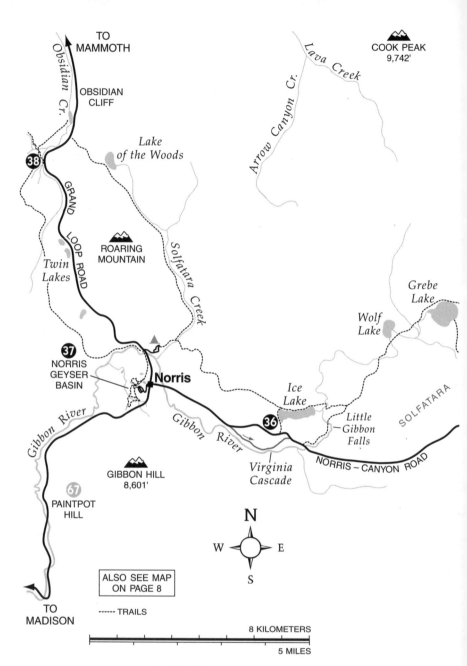

TO
MAMMOTH

Obsidian Cr.

OBSIDIAN
CLIFF

38

GRAND LOOP ROAD

*Lake
of the Woods*

ROARING
MOUNTAIN

*Twin
Lakes*

Solfatara Creek

37

NORRIS
GEYSER
BASIN

Norris

Gibbon River

Gibbon River

36

*Ice
Lake*

Arrow Canyon Cr.

Lava Creek

COOK PEAK
9,742'

*Grebe
Lake*

*Wolf
Lake*

SOLFATARA

*Little
Gibbon
Falls*

NORRIS – CANYON ROAD

*Virginia
Cascade*

67

PAINTPOT
HILL

GIBBON HILL
8,601'

N

W ⊕ E

S

ALSO SEE MAP
ON PAGE 8

----- TRAILS

TO
MADISON

8 KILOMETERS

5 MILES

HIKES 29–39
CANYON – NORRIS

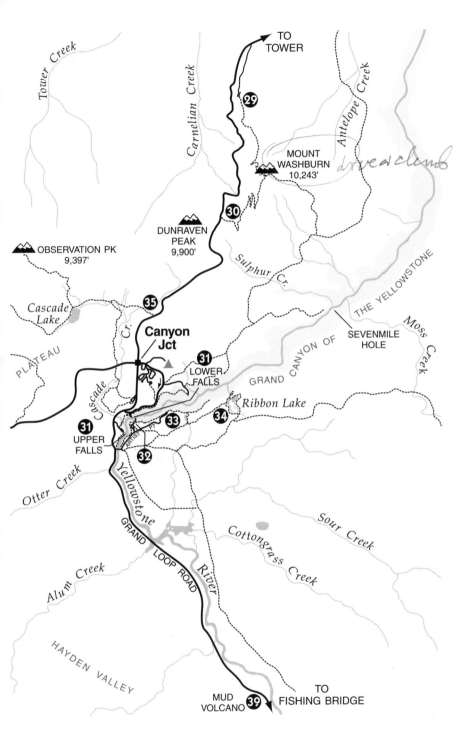

TO TOWER

Tower Creek

Carnelian Creek

Antelope Creek

29

MOUNT WASHBURN
10,243'

drove a climb

30

DUNRAVEN PEAK
9,900'

OBSERVATION PK
9,397'

Sulphur Cr.

THE YELLOWSTONE

Moss Creek

35

Cascade Lake

PLATEAU

Cascade Cr.

SEVENMILE HOLE

Canyon Jct

31

LOWER FALLS

GRAND CANYON OF

Ribbon Lake

33

34

Cascade

31

UPPER FALLS

ARTIST

32

Otter Creek

Yellowstone

Sour Creek

GRAND LOOP ROAD

River

Cottongrass Creek

Alum Creek

HAYDEN VALLEY

MUD VOLCANO

39

TO FISHING BRIDGE

Hike 29
Mount Washburn
FROM THE CHITTENDEN ROAD TRAIL

Hiking distance: 5.6 miles round trip
Hiking time: 3 hours
Elevation gain: 1,500 feet
Maps: U.S.G.S. Mount Washburn
       Trails Illustrated Tower/Canyon

map
next page

Summary of hike: The Chittenden Road Trail is one of three trails to the summit of Mount Washburn. This route, an old wagon road, approaches the summit on an easy grade from the north. The trail follows a long, exposed alpine ridge covered with wildflowers. Large numbers of bighorn sheep pasture on these upper mountain slopes. Near the 10,243-foot summit the three trails merge, leading to the fire lookout tower and viewing platform. The 360-degree panoramic views of the Yellowstone Plateau and surrounding mountains are tremendous, extending to Yellowstone Lake, the Grand Canyon of the Yellowstone, Hayden Valley, the Grand Tetons, and the many geyser basins. Below the lookout tower is a glass-enclosed observation room and interpretive center with a telescope.

Driving directions: From Canyon, drive 9.7 miles towards Tower to the signed Chittenden Road turnoff on the right. Turn right and continue 1.4 miles on the gravel road to the trailhead parking area at the end of the road.

From Tower Junction, drive 8.5 miles towards Canyon to the signed Chittenden Road on the left. Follow the directions above.

Hiking directions: Head south up the wide, rock-lined trail, overlooking the massive valley on the left. Climb up the ridge and merge with the Chittenden Road Trail. Take the narrow service road gradually but steadily uphill, alternating between meadows and forested groves. At 0.7 miles, the path curves left, opening up views of Dunraven Peak and the lookout tower.

Traverse the west flank of Mount Washburn, crossing the flower-filled alpine landscape and overlooking the burn area of the 1988 fires. The road zigzags up to a saddle and a 3-way intersection near the top. The Washburn Spur Trail descends left (east) to Washburn Hot Springs and Canyon, while the Mount Washburn Trail from Dunraven Pass (Hike 30) descends to the south. Make a sharp hairpin turn on the right fork, heading west a short distance to the summit and lookout tower. After marveling at the views, return along the same trail.

Hike 30
Mount Washburn Trail ✕
FROM DUNRAVEN PASS

Hiking distance: 6.4 miles round trip
Hiking time: 3.5 hours
Elevation gain: 1,400 feet
Maps: U.S.G.S. Mount Washburn
       Trails Illustrated Tower/Canyon

map
next page

Summary of hike: The Mount Washburn Trail from Dunraven Pass is one of three trails to the summit of Mount Washburn, the cone of an ancient volcano. The trail is a turn-of-the-century wagon road that approaches the summit from the southwest. The broad alpine slopes of the mountain are filled with a magnificent display of wildflowers, rivaling any display in the park. The upper slopes are a summer pasture for bighorn sheep. Perched on the 10,243-foot summit is the fire lookout tower and viewing platform. The incredible, sweeping 360-degree panoramic vistas include the Yellowstone Plateau and surrounding mountains, Yellowstone Lake, the Grand Canyon of the Yellowstone, Hayden Valley, the Grand Tetons, and several distant geyser basins. Below the tower is a glass-enclosed observation room with a telescope.

Driving directions: From Canyon, drive 4.8 miles towards Tower to the signed Mount Washburn Trail on the right at Dunraven Pass. Turn right and park in the parking lot.

From Tower Junction, drive 13.4 miles towards Canyon to the signed trailhead on the left.

Hiking directions: Take the wide, signed trail up the southern flank of Mount Washburn. Views open up immediately of Dunraven Peak, the Grand Canyon of the Yellowstone, and the Grand Tetons. At 0.6 miles, a horseshoe bend curves to the north past lava rock outcroppings. The fire lookout can be seen at the summit of Mount Washburn. Enter the forested canyon, and begin a series of long switchbacks that ascend the mountain. Continue uphill through the pine, spruce, and fir forest. Near the top, the path emerges from the forest. Follow the narrow exposed ridge across the fragile subalpine tundra. At the top of the ridge is a wide, 3-way intersection. The Washburn Spur Trail descends to the right to Washburn Hot Springs and Canyon. The Chittenden Road Trail (Hike 29) descends to the north. Take the left fork, heading west a short distance to the lookout tower and observation room at the summit. After enjoying the vistas, return along the same route.

HIKES 29 • 30
MOUNT WASHBURN
from CHITTENDEN ROAD TRAIL
and DUNRAVEN PASS

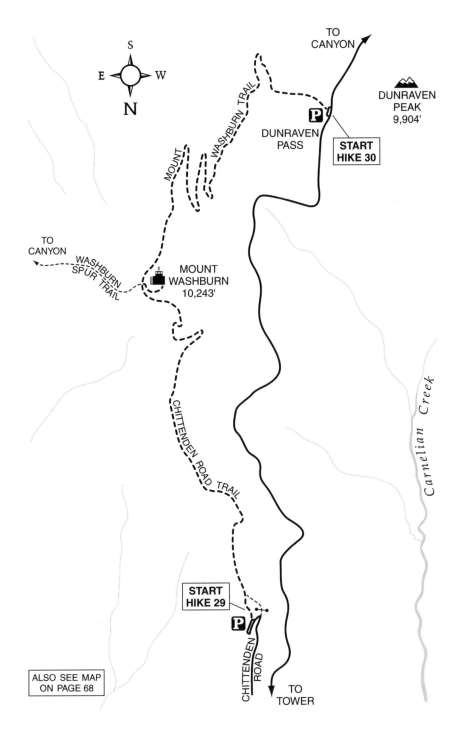

TO
CANYON

S

E — W

N

DUNRAVEN
PEAK
9,904'

MOUNT WASHBURN TRAIL

P
DUNRAVEN
PASS

**START
HIKE 30**

TO
CANYON

WASHBURN
SPUR TRAIL

MOUNT
WASHBURN
10,243'

Carnelian Creek

CHITTENDEN ROAD TRAIL

**START
HIKE 29**

P

CHITTENDEN ROAD

TO
TOWER

ALSO SEE MAP
ON PAGE 68

Hike 31
Upper Falls, Lower Falls, and Crystal Falls
GRAND CANYON OF THE YELLOWSTONE

Hiking distance: 3 miles round trip
Hiking time: 2 hours
Elevation gain: 600 feet
Maps: U.S.G.S. Canyon Village
Trails Illustrated Mammoth Hot Springs, Tower/Canyon
The Yellowstone Association Canyon map

Summary of hike: This hike explores three magnificent waterfalls in the Grand Canyon of the Yellowstone, including the two most famous waterfalls of the park. The trail leads to excellent vantage points of both Upper Falls, at the head of the Grand Canyon of the Yellowstone with a 109-foot drop, and Lower Falls, the tallest waterfall in Yellowstone with a 308-foot drop (cover photo). Crystal Falls lies between the two thunderous cataracts on Cascade Creek, with a three-tiered, 129-foot drop. A footbridge crosses over Cascade Creek just above Crystal Falls. For an awesome view of Lower Falls, follow the Brink of Falls Trail as it steeply descends 600 feet into the canyon to the top of the falls, where the Yellowstone River plunges straight down over a notch in the rock wall.

Driving directions: From Canyon Junction, drive 1.6 miles south towards Fishing Bridge to the Upper Falls spur road on the left. Continue 0.2 miles and park in the lot. (See map on p. 79.)

Hiking directions: From the parking lot and restrooms, walk back along the side of the road about 200 yards to the North Rim Trail on the right. Take this trail a short distance to the canyon rim. From the rim is an excellent view of Crystal Falls. Continue on the trail towards the falls, and cross the footbridge over Cascade Creek. After crossing the bridge, several short trails to the right of the main trail lead to overlooks from the top of the falls. Continue along the main trail, which follows the rim of the canyon, to another footbridge on the left. Cross the bridge. The trail joins the Brink of Falls Trail and descends via switchbacks to the Lower Falls overlook at the very top of this magnificent falls. The force of the river can literally be felt. To return, take the same path back.

Back at the parking lot, take the trail to the southeast for a short quarter-mile round trip walk to the brink of Upper Falls, which plunges 109 feet over a rock lip.

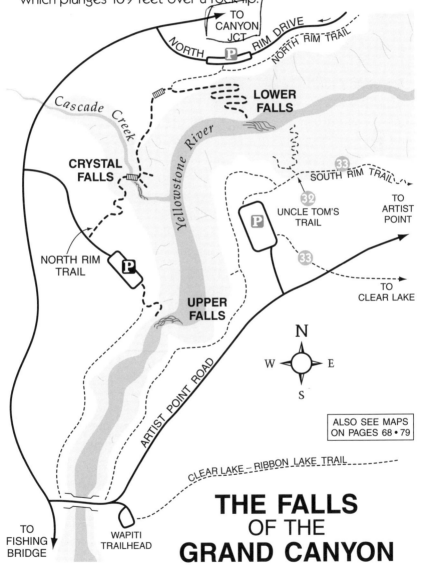

TO CANYON JCT

NORTH RIM DRIVE

NORTH RIM TRAIL

Cascade Creek

LOWER FALLS

CRYSTAL FALLS

Yellowstone River

33

SOUTH RIM TRAIL

32

UNCLE TOM'S TRAIL

TO ARTIST POINT

33

TO CLEAR LAKE

NORTH RIM TRAIL

UPPER FALLS

N

W ← → E

S

ALSO SEE MAPS ON PAGES 68 • 79

ARTIST POINT ROAD

CLEAR LAKE – RIBBON LAKE TRAIL

THE FALLS
OF THE
GRAND CANYON

TO FISHING BRIDGE

WAPITI TRAILHEAD

Hike 32
Uncle Tom's Trail
GRAND CANYON OF THE YELLOWSTONE

Hiking distance: 1 mile round trip
Hiking time: 1 hour
Elevation gain: 500 feet
Maps: U.S.G.S. Canyon Village
Trails Illustrated Tower/Canyon
The Yellowstone Association Canyon map

Summary of hike: From 1898 to 1903, "Uncle" Tom Richardson took park visitors 500 feet into the canyon on a series of precarious stairs and rope ladders for a spectacular view of Lower Falls. This unusual trail, named in his honor, now utilizes a steep metal stairway bolted into the canyon wall, leading into the depths of the Grand Canyon of the Yellowstone. These sturdy steps take you to an overwhelming close-up view of the canyon at the base of the crashing 308-foot Lower Falls, one of the greatest waterfalls in North America and the largest in Yellowstone National Park (cover photo). The trail offers close, interior views of the rock spires and hoodoos in the eroded canyon walls. This hike is strenuous and not recommended for everyone.

Driving directions: From Canyon Junction, drive 2.2 miles south towards Fishing Bridge. Turn left on Artist Point Road. Continue 0.6 miles to Uncle Tom's parking area on the left. Turn left and park. (See map on page 79.)

Hiking directions: From the far north end of the parking lot, take the trail north towards the canyon rim, then bear to the right. The trail descends via switchbacks to the stairs. Head down the 328 metal stairs leading into the canyon to the base of Lower Falls, where the dramatic power of the roaring water can be felt. Return to the trailhead back up the stairs.

The Brink of Falls Trail to the top of Lower Falls can be seen across the canyon (Hike 31).

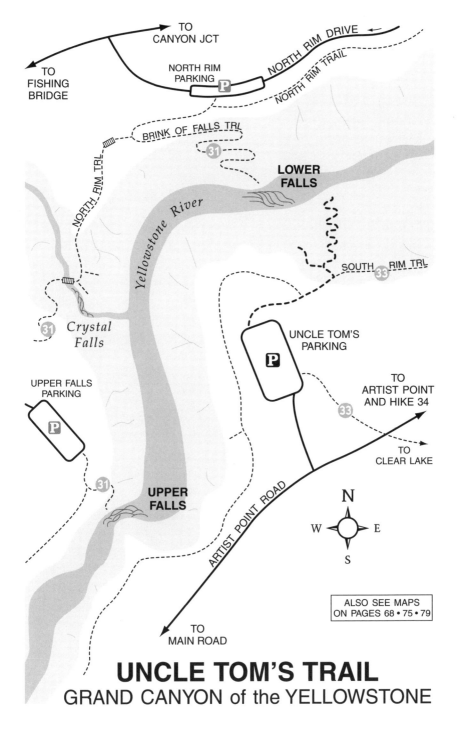

TO
CANYON JCT

TO
FISHING
BRIDGE

NORTH RIM
PARKING 🅿

NORTH RIM DRIVE

NORTH RIM TRAIL

BRINK OF FALLS TRL

NORTH RIM TRL

31

LOWER
FALLS

Yellowstone River

SOUTH RIM TRL

33

31 Crystal
Falls

UNCLE TOM'S
PARKING
🅿

TO
ARTIST POINT
AND HIKE 34

33

UPPER FALLS
PARKING
🅿

TO
CLEAR LAKE

31

UPPER
FALLS

ARTIST POINT ROAD

N
W ✦ E
S

ALSO SEE MAPS
ON PAGES 68 • 75 • 79

TO
MAIN ROAD

UNCLE TOM'S TRAIL
GRAND CANYON of the YELLOWSTONE

Hike 33
South Rim—Clear Lake Loop
GRAND CANYON OF THE YELLOWSTONE

Hiking distance: 3 miles round trip
Hiking time: 2 hours
Elevation gain: Near-level
Maps: U.S.G.S. Canyon Village
       Trails Illustrated Tower/Canyon
       The Yellowstone Association Canyon map

Summary of hike: This near-level trail follows the rim of the Grand Canyon of the Yellowstone. The trail overlooks the steep canyon and its two thundering waterfalls—Upper and Lower Falls (Hike 31). The trail passes Lily Pad Lake en route to the spring-fed Clear Lake, completely surrounded by forest in an active thermal area containing boiling water holes and bubbling mud pots. This is a magnificent hike with a variety of scenery and geological features.

Driving directions: Same as Hike 32.

Hiking directions: From the parking area, walk north towards the canyon. Curve to the right (east) along the rim towards Artist Point, passing Uncle Tom's Trail (Hike 32). The trail reenters civilization at the Artist Point parking lot. Pick the trail back up at the end of the lot. From Artist Point, continue east along the rim to Lily Pad Lake, a half mile ahead. After passing Lily Pad Lake there is a trail junction. Take the right fork to Clear Lake. (The left fork leads to Ribbon Lake, Hike 34.) Approximately 200 feet ahead is the beginning of the mud pots, fumaroles, and thermal pool area. This display of thermal activity continues through the barren landscape to Clear Lake. Shortly after passing Clear Lake is a trail junction in a meadow. The left fork continues to the Wapiti trailhead. Take the right fork back to Uncle Tom's parking area.

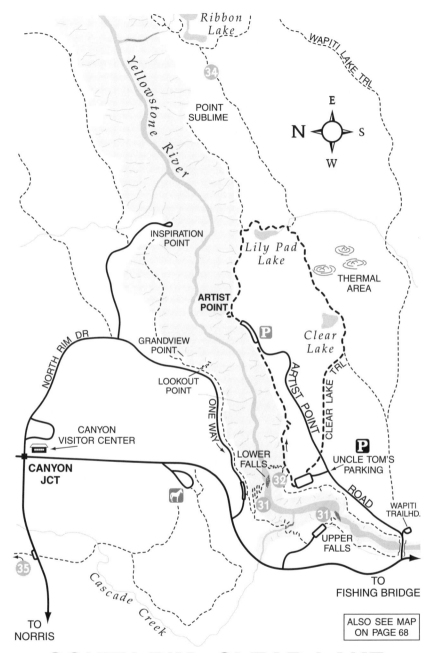

Ribbon Lake

34

POINT SUBLIME

WAPITI LAKE TRL

E
N — S
W

Yellowstone River

INSPIRATION POINT

Lily Pad Lake

THERMAL AREA

ARTIST POINT

P

Clear Lake

NORTH RIM DR

GRANDVIEW POINT

LOOKOUT POINT

ARTIST POINT

CLEAR LAKE TRL

CANYON VISITOR CENTER

ONE WAY

CANYON JCT

LOWER FALLS

P
UNCLE TOM'S PARKING

32

ROAD

WAPITI TRAILHD.

31

31

UPPER FALLS

35

Cascade Creek

TO FISHING BRIDGE

TO NORRIS

ALSO SEE MAP ON PAGE 68

SOUTH RIM—CLEAR LAKE
GRAND CANYON of the YELLOWSTONE

Hike 34
Ribbon Lake and Silver Cord Cascade
GRAND CANYON OF THE YELLOWSTONE

Hiking distance: 4.2 miles round trip
Hiking time: 2 hours
Elevation gain: 300 feet
Maps: U.S.G.S. Canyon Village
　　　　Trails Illustrated Tower/Canyon
　　　　The Yellowstone Association Canyon map

Summary of hike: Ribbon Lake is actually two lakes that sit in a grassy meadow joined by a short, shallow stream. Surface Creek flows through Ribbon Lake en route to the Grand Canyon of the Yellowstone, then tumbles down Silver Cord Cascade, a narrow 1,200-foot cascade dropping through a thin crevice in the canyon wall. The hike to Ribbon Lake begins at Artist Point, an overlook of Lower Falls framed by the Grand Canyon (cover photo). The first part of the trail follows the edge of the Grand Canyon of the Yellowstone high above the river. Just beyond Ribbon Lake is an overlook by Silver Cord Cascade.

Driving directions: From Canyon Junction, drive 2.2 miles south towards Yellowstone Lake. Turn left on Artist Point Road. Continue 1.5 miles to the Artist Point parking lot at the road's end. (See map on page 79.)

Hiking directions: Hike east on the paved path along the rim of the Grand Canyon of the Yellowstone. A short distance ahead is Artist Point—an overlook of the canyon and Lower Falls. Take the path to the right uphill towards Point Sublime. The trail follows the rim of the canyon for a half mile, then curves south and enters the forest. At 0.8 miles, cross a boardwalk over a marshy meadow to a trail fork at the south end of Lily Pad Lake. Take the left fork through the forest to a trail intersection by Ribbon Lake. Continue straight ahead. Bear left at another trail split, and head to the Silver Cord Cascade overlook at a rocky point on the canyon's rim. The main trail loops around Ribbon Lake. To return, reverse your route.

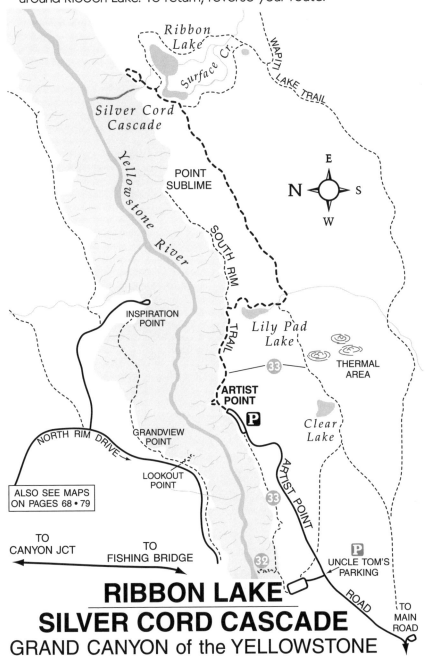

Ribbon Lake

Surface Cr.

WAPITI LAKE TRAIL

Silver Cord Cascade

POINT SUBLIME

E
N — S
W

Yellowstone River

SOUTH RIM TRAIL

INSPIRATION POINT

Lily Pad Lake

33

THERMAL AREA

ARTIST POINT

P

Clear Lake

NORTH RIM DRIVE

GRANDVIEW POINT

LOOKOUT POINT

ARTIST POINT ROAD

ALSO SEE MAPS ON PAGES 68 • 79

33

TO CANYON JCT

TO FISHING BRIDGE

32

P
UNCLE TOM'S PARKING

ROAD

TO MAIN ROAD

RIBBON LAKE
SILVER CORD CASCADE
GRAND CANYON of the YELLOWSTONE

Hike 35
Cascade Lake Trail

Hiking distance: 5 miles round trip
Hiking time: 2.5 hours
Elevation gain: Level
Maps: U.S.G.S. Cook Peak, Mount Washburn, and Crystal Falls
        Trails Illustrated Mammoth Hot Springs, Tower/Canyon

Summary of hike: Cascade Lake sits in a natural depression on the Solfatara Plateau at the base of Observation Peak. The Cascade Lake Trail winds through large open meadows covered in wildflowers, stands of lodgepole pines, and across numerous streams and footbridges. Views of the surrounding mountains lie on the distant horizon. The last half of the hike parallels Cascade Creek to the north shore of the 36-acre lake. Moose, bison, and grizzly bear frequent this area. Check with the rangers about bear activity before heading into the back-country.

Driving directions: From Canyon Junction, drive 1.3 miles north towards Tower to the Cascade Lake Picnic Area on the left. Turn left and park in any picnic pullout area.

Hiking directions: The trailhead is on the far west end of the Cascade Lake Picnic Area. Take the well-defined trail, and head west through an old lodgepole pine forest to the open meadows. Skirt the edge of the forest through the meadow, frequently crossing over streams on footbridges and logs. At one mile, in a narrow forest pocket, is a junction on the left with the Cascade Creek Trail. (This trail is another route to Cascade Lake, beginning 1.7 miles south on the road between Canyon and Norris. The signed trailhead is a half mile west of Canyon.) Stay to the right and continue west through lodgepole pine, spruce, and fir, parallel but away from Cascade Creek. As you near the lake, the path opens into an expansive grassy meadow. The path reaches the north shore of Cascade Lake at the far end of the meadow. Short side paths lead to the shoreline. This is our turnaround spot.

To hike further, the trail continues 2 miles west along the Solfatara Plateau to Grebe Lake. The north trail to Observation Peak climbs 3 miles and 1,400 feet to the summit.

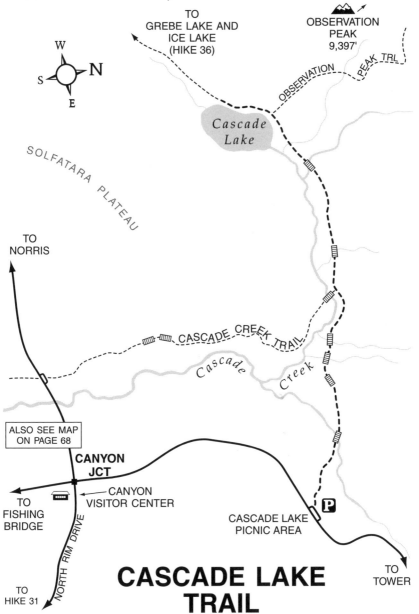

Hike 36
Ice Lake and Little Gibbon Falls Loop

Hiking distance: 4.5 mile loop
Hiking time: 2 hours
Elevation gain: 150 feet
Maps: U.S.G.S. Norris Junction and Crystal Falls
       Trails Illustrated Mammoth Hot Springs

Summary of hike: Ice Lake is a long, narrow 224-acre lake surrounded by lodgepole pines on the Solfatara Plateau. The Ice Lake Loop is an easy, incredibly diverse, and lightly used hiking trail. Ice Lake is reached within minutes of the trailhead. The path continues to 25-foot Little Gibbon Falls, a smaller version of the 84-foot Gibbon Falls between Madison and Norris. The trail follows the cascading Gibbon River through a small canyon to Virginia Meadows, a beautiful pastoral meadow along a stretch of the meandering river. Part of the hike passes through a burn area from the 1988 fires, the ground now blanketed with a new-growth pine forest.

Driving directions: The Ice Lake trailhead parking area is located 8.2 miles west of Canyon Junction and 3.4 miles east of Norris. The turnout is on the north side of the road.

Hiking directions: From the parking pullout, head north across a wooden bridge into the lodgepole pine forest to a trail split a short distance ahead. Bear to the left, along the west side of Ice Lake, to a junction with the Howard Eaton Trail. Take the right fork along the north shore of the lake. Continue past the lake to a crossing of the Gibbon River. Downfall logs can be used to cross. At 2.3 miles is a junction with the Wolf Lake Trail. Take the right fork towards Little Gibbon Falls. As you approach the cascading Gibbon River, the trail descends to a small canyon. Use a log to cross the river, and climb the ridge to an overlook of Little Gibbon Falls. Follow the canyon and river southwest into Virginia Meadows. Hike through the meadows and back to the highway, a half mile east of the trailhead. Follow the road to the right, completing the loop.

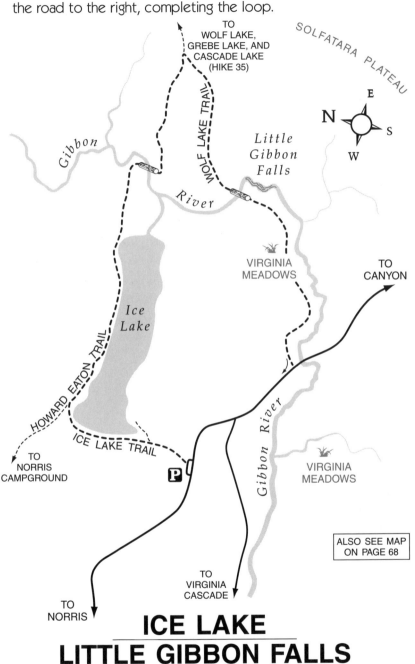

TO WOLF LAKE, GREBE LAKE, AND CASCADE LAKE (HIKE 35)

WOLF LAKE TRAIL

SOLFATARA PLATEAU

Gibbon

Little Gibbon Falls

N E S W

River

VIRGINIA MEADOWS

TO CANYON

Ice Lake

HOWARD EATON TRAIL

ICE LAKE TRAIL

Gibbon River

VIRGINIA MEADOWS

TO NORRIS CAMPGROUND

P

ALSO SEE MAP ON PAGE 68

TO VIRGINIA CASCADE

TO NORRIS

ICE LAKE
LITTLE GIBBON FALLS

Hike 37
Norris Geyser Basin

Hiking distance: 2 mile double loop
Hiking time: 1.5 hours
Elevation gain: 100 feet
Maps: U.S.G.S. Norris Junction
      Trails Illustrated Mammoth Hot Springs
      Yellowstone Association Norris Geyser Basin map

Summary of hike: Norris Geyser Basin is the oldest and hottest geyser basin in Yellowstone. The highly acidic water has created a stark, barren landscape. Two distinctly different basins make up the Norris Geyser Basin. A loop trail explores each one, comprised of a series of boardwalks, paths, and overlooks. The Back Basin has several impressive geysers, including Echinus Geyser, which erupts in intervals ranging from 20—80 minutes and shoots 70—125 feet high, and Steamboat Geyser, the tallest geyser in the world, with 300- to 400-foot eruptions. The Porcelain Basin has hot springs, steam vents, and pools. Both basins funnel water into Tantalus Creek, which joins the Gibbon River. The loops begin and end at the Norris Geyser Basin Museum. From the museum is an overlook of the colorful and expansive Porcelain Basin.

Driving directions: From Norris, drive 0.4 miles west on the Norris Geyser Basin Road to the parking lot at road's end.

Hiking directions: Hike west on the paved path to the bookstore and museum. From the museum, take the left fork, heading south on the Back Basin Trail. Head left across a series of wooden walkways and overlooks to a trail split. The right fork is a cut-across for a shorter loop. The left fork leads to viewing platforms for Echinus Geyser. The trail continues past a variety of geysers and caldrons, returning to the west side of the museum at an overlook. Begin the loop around Porcelain Basin on the left fork, heading downhill into the pine forest. The trail crosses the stark but colorful basin on a wooden boardwalk. After looping through the basin, take the left fork at a junction up to the Porcelain Terrace Overlook. From the overlook, the trail curves to the right, completing the loop back at the museum.

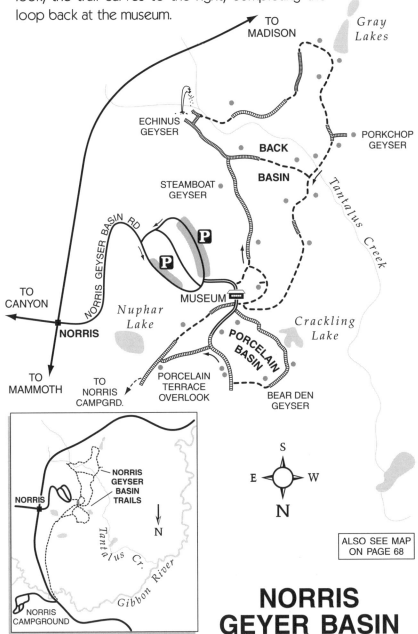

TO MADISON

Gray Lakes

ECHINUS GEYSER

PORKCHOP GEYSER

BACK

BASIN

STEAMBOAT GEYSER

Tantalus Creek

NORRIS GEYSER BASIN RD

TO CANYON

NORRIS

Nuphar Lake

MUSEUM

Crackling Lake

PORCELAIN BASIN

TO MAMMOTH

TO NORRIS CAMPGRD.

PORCELAIN TERRACE OVERLOOK

BEAR DEN GEYSER

NORRIS GEYSER BASIN TRAILS

NORRIS

Tantalus Cr.

N

Gibbon River

NORRIS CAMPGROUND

S

E — W

N

ALSO SEE MAP ON PAGE 68

NORRIS GEYER BASIN

Hike 38
Grizzly Lake

Hiking distance: 3.6 miles round trip
Hiking time: 2 hours
Elevation gain: 400 feet
Maps: U.S.G.S. Obsidian Cliff and Mount Holmes
Trails Illustrated Mammoth Hot Springs

Summary of hike: Grizzly Lake is a gorgeous 136-acre lake nestled in a valley between two 300-foot ridges. The long and narrow lake is bordered by spruce, fir, and lodgepole pines. It is fed by Straight Creek, which enters the lake from the south and exits to the north. The trail climbs to the west-facing ridge and descends to the lake in the valley. Atop the ridge are magnificent views of mile-long Grizzly Lake, Mount Holmes, Trilobite Point, Dome Mountain, and Antler Peak. The trail passes through a burn area from the 1976 and 1988 fires, now blanketed with a new growth of the future forest.

Driving directions: From Norris, drive 6.2 miles north towards Mammoth to the signed parking pullout on the left.

From Mammoth, drive 14.8 miles south towards Norris to the signed parking pullout on the right.

Hiking directions: The trail heads north, parallel to the road for a short distance. Cross a wooden bridge over Obsidian Creek, and wind through the open meadow, crossing two more bridges en route. At the west end of the meadow, switchbacks lead 250 feet up the hill. From the ridge, traverse the hillside up the draw. Beyond the draw, the trail crosses a series of meadows and rolling hills to an overlook at 1.4 miles. Begin a switchbacking descent, dropping 300 feet to the north end of Grizzly Lake. Continue around the tip of the lake to Straight Creek, the inlet stream of the lake. This is the turnaround point for the hike. To hike further, the trail continues along Straight Creek to a junction with the Mount Holmes Trail. From the junction, the trail climbs 8 miles to Mount Holmes.

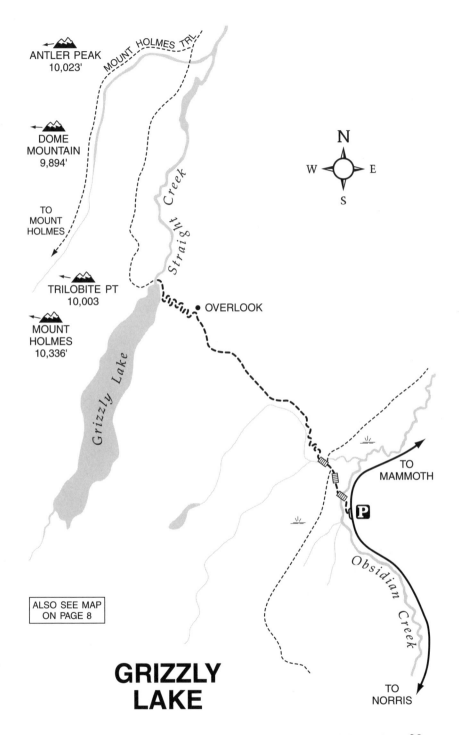

ANTLER PEAK
10,023'

MOUNT HOLMES TRL.

DOME
MOUNTAIN
9,894'

TO
MOUNT
HOLMES

Straight Creek

TRILOBITE PT
10,003

MOUNT
HOLMES
10,336'

Grizzly Lake

• OVERLOOK

N
W E
S

TO
MAMMOTH

P

Obsidian Creek

ALSO SEE MAP
ON PAGE 8

GRIZZLY
LAKE

TO
NORRIS

Hike 39
Mud Volcano

Hiking distance: 0.7 mile loop
Hiking time: 30 minutes
Elevation gain: 200 feet
Maps: U.S.G.S. Lake and Canyon Village
Trails Illustrated Yellowstone Lake
The Yellowstone Association Mud Volcano Trail Guide

Summary of hike: Mud Volcano is located just north of Yellowstone Lake between Canyon and Fishing Bridge. The barren landscape is filled with pools of thick mud, bubbling clay caldrons, geysers, hot springs, steam vents rich in sulfuric acid, and the pungent aroma of hydrogen sulfide. A 0.7-mile loop of trails and boardwalks winds around several diverse hydrothermal features, including the turbulent Mud Volcano crater, rising 30-feet high and spreading 30-feet wide; Mud Caldron and Black Dragon's Caldron, seething masses of bubbling mud pools; Dragon's Mouth Spring, a splashing, belching spring that fills a cave on the hillside; and the steaming, odoriferous cones of Grizzly Fumarole.

Driving directions: Mud Volcano is on the road between Canyon and Fishing Bridge. The well-signed parking lot is on the west side of the road, 10 miles south from Canyon and 5.8 miles north from Fishing Bridge .

Hiking directions: Begin the loop at the far south end of the parking lot. Cross the bridge over the outlet stream from Mud Caldron. Ascend Cooking Hillside, overlooking Mud Geyser (the large mud pool) and numerous fumaroles. Pass Sizzling Basin and Churning Caldron to a junction atop the plateau. A spur path on the left leads to an overlook of Black Dragon's Caldron and Sour Lake. The main loop strolls through an open woodland to Grizzly Fumarole. Descend steps to the vigorously boiling Mud Volcano and Dragon's Mouth Spring.

Return to the parking lot by Mud Caldron. A short walk across the highway is the fragrant, spewing waters of Sulfur Caldron.

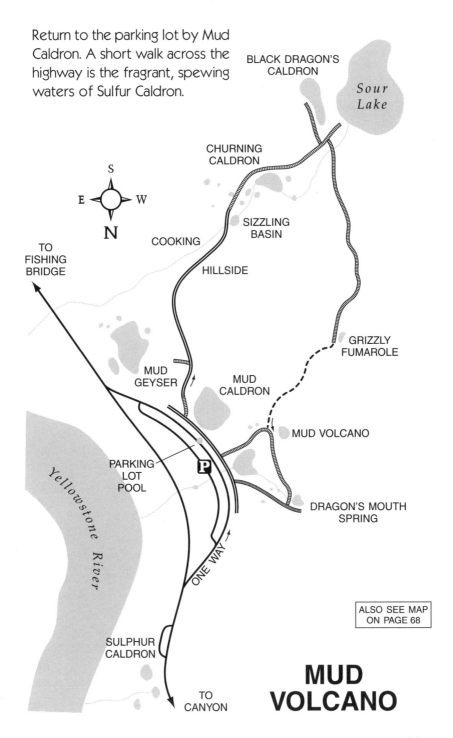

BLACK DRAGON'S CALDRON

Sour Lake

CHURNING CALDRON

SIZZLING BASIN

S

E ⊕ W

N

COOKING

TO FISHING BRIDGE

HILLSIDE

GRIZZLY FUMAROLE

MUD GEYSER

MUD CALDRON

MUD VOLCANO

PARKING LOT POOL

P

DRAGON'S MOUTH SPRING

Yellowstone River

ONE WAY

ALSO SEE MAP ON PAGE 68

SULPHUR CALDRON

TO CANYON

MUD VOLCANO

Hike 40
Pahaska—Sunlight Trail to Sam Berry Meadow

Hiking distance: 7 miles round trip
Hiking time: 3.5 hours
Elevation gain: 250 feet
Maps: U.S.G.S. Pahaska Tepee

Summary of hike: The Pahaska–Sunlight Trail is an 18-mile trail beginning at the North Fork Shoshoni River near Pahaska Tepee, just outside the east Yellowstone entrance. The trail heads north, eventually leading through Camp Monaco, a hunting camp established in 1913 by Buffalo Bill Cody during a trip with the Prince of Monaco. The trail ends in Sunlight Basin, the next major drainage to the north. This hike follows the first 3.5 miles of the trail along the North Fork Shoshoni River to Sam Berry Meadow. The grassy meadow sits on the banks of the river fringed with spruce and pines and has a primitive campsite. The trail includes magnificent views of the surrounding peaks and the Sleeping Giant Winter Sports Area.

Driving directions: From the east entrance station of Yellowstone, drive east out of the park for 3.3 miles to the signed Pahaska–Sunlight Trailhead on the left, located 1.1 miles past Pahaska Tepee. Turn left and drive 0.1 mile to the trailhead parking area.
   From Cody, drive west on Highway 14–16–20 for 41.4 miles.

Hiking directions: Hike north past the trailhead sign and head uphill, entering a lodgepole pine and Douglas fir forest. Wind through the forest with panoramic views of the surrounding peaks. Cross small feeder streams. At 1.1 miles, the trail descends to the North Fork Shoshone River and a T-junction. Take the right fork upstream past a junction with the Crow Creek Trail on the left. Stay right, following the level watercourse through the burn area from the Clover Mist fire of 1988, which can be seen far up the meadow. At 3.5 miles, the trail

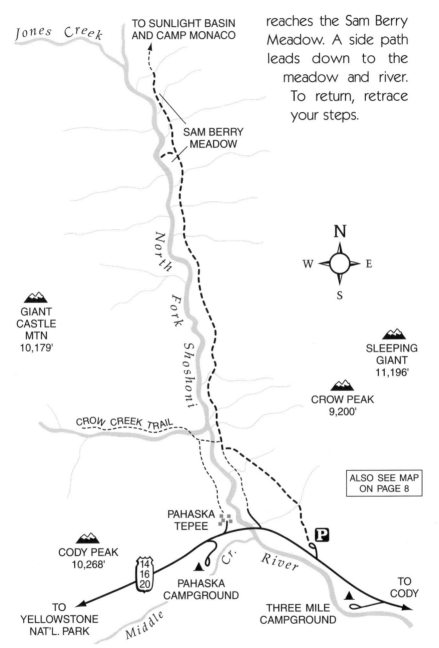

reaches the Sam Berry Meadow. A side path leads down to the meadow and river. To return, retrace your steps.

TO SUNLIGHT BASIN AND CAMP MONACO

Jones Creek

SAM BERRY MEADOW

N
W   E
S

North Fork Shoshoni

GIANT CASTLE MTN 10,179'

SLEEPING GIANT 11,196'

CROW PEAK 9,200'

CROW CREEK TRAIL

ALSO SEE MAP ON PAGE 8

PAHASKA TEPEE

P

CODY PEAK 10,268'

14 16 20

Cr.

River

PAHASKA CAMPGROUND

THREE MILE CAMPGROUND

TO CODY

TO YELLOWSTONE NAT'L. PARK

Middle

PAHASKA-SUNLIGHT TRAIL

Hike 41
Storm Point Loop

Hiking distance: 2.5 mile loop
Hiking time: 1.5 hours
Elevation gain: Near-level
Maps: U.S.G.S. Lake Butte
       Trails Illustrated Yellowstone Lake

map
next page

Summary of hike: Storm Point is a tree-covered rocky bluff at the west tip of Mary Bay on the north shore of Yellowstone Lake. From the storm-battered point are sweeping vistas across the 87,450-acre lake, the largest alpine lake in North America. The lakefront views include Stevenson Island, the Red Mountains, and the Grand Tetons. The Storm Point Loop Trail passes 24-acre Indian Pond, a circular crater created by an ancient hydrothermal explosion. The pond was a historic camping site for Indians. With its close proximity to Yellowstone Lake, it currently plays host to a variety of shorebirds and lies along a corridor for moose, bison, and grizzly bears. The trail leads past Indian Pond and follows the shoreline bluffs through forests and meadows to Storm Point.

Driving directions: From the Fishing Bridge Visitor Center, drive 2.5 miles east towards the east park entrance. The turnout and trailhead are on the right.

Hiking directions: From the parking turnout, the trail heads south through a meadow towards Yellowstone Lake. Within minutes is the north edge of Indian Pond, an ancient volcanic crater. The trail leads along the pond's west shore to Yellowstone Lake. From Yellowstone Lake, follow the shoreline bluffs, heading south as it weaves in and out of the lodgepole forest. At one mile, the trail reaches the rocky bluffs of Storm Point. A spur trail to the left leads to the point.

After exploring the rock peninsula of Storm Point, begin the return along the shoreline bluffs. In a few minutes, the trail curves away from the shore through an old, dense lodgepole pine forest to the north. From this forest, emerge back into the sagebrush flat, cross a creek, and head east towards Indian Pond to complete the loop.

Hike 42
Pelican Creek Nature Trail

Hiking distance: 1 mile loop
Hiking time: 30 minutes
Elevation gain: Level
Maps: U.S.G.S. Lake Butte
Trails Illustrated Yellowstone Lake

map
next page

Summary of hike: Pelican Creek empties into Yellowstone Lake on its northeast shore between Fishing Bridge and Storm Point, in close proximity to the riverhead of the Yellowstone River. Pelican Creek, the largest tributary stream of Yellowstone Lake, twists and turns through Pelican Valley on its journey to the lake. The Pelican Creek Nature Trail follows the creek to its southern terminus, where it joins the lake. The short, easy trail crosses a meadow and winds through a lodgepole pine, spruce, and fir forest en route to a beautiful obsidian-sand beach. From the beach are views of Stevenson Island and Mount Sheridan to the southwest.

Driving directions: From Fishing Bridge Junction, drive 1.5 miles east towards the east park entrance. The signed trailhead parking area is on the right.

Hiking directions: From the parking area, hike south through the lush lodgepole pine forest towards Yellowstone Lake. The loop begins thirty feet from the trailhead. Go to the right through the grove and meadows. At 0.4 miles is a trail fork. The right fork leads a few feet to Yellowstone Lake and a long sandy beach. The left fork continues east on the loop, paralleling the shore to another trail split. The left fork heads into the forest and fades out. Take the right fork down to the sandy beach. From the beach at the mouth of the creek, curve back into the forest, parallel to Pelican Creek. Cross a long wooden walkway through the grassy wetlands, completing the loop near the trailhead.

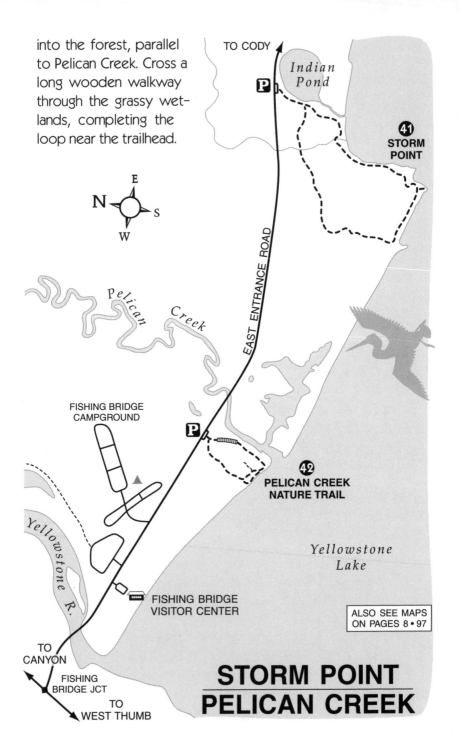

TO CODY

Indian Pond

P

41
STORM POINT

N ◆ E / S / W

EAST ENTRANCE ROAD

Pelican Creek

FISHING BRIDGE CAMPGROUND

P

42
PELICAN CREEK NATURE TRAIL

Yellowstone Lake

Yellowstone R.

FISHING BRIDGE VISITOR CENTER

ALSO SEE MAPS ON PAGES 8 • 97

TO CANYON

FISHING BRIDGE JCT

TO WEST THUMB

STORM POINT
PELICAN CREEK

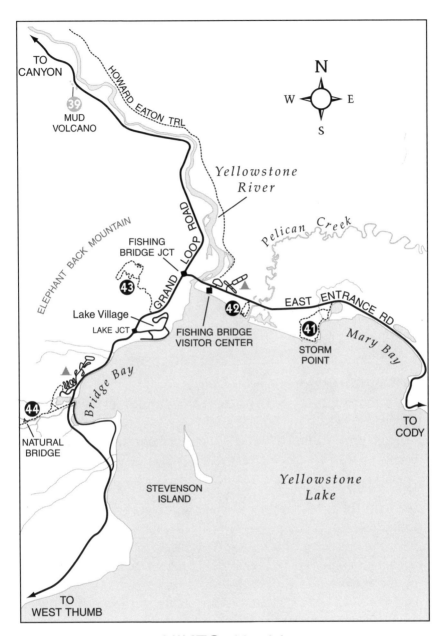

HIKES 41–44
FISHING BRIDGE
NORTH YELLOWSTONE LAKE

Hike 43
Elephant Back Loop

Hiking distance: 4 miles round trip
Hiking time: 2 hours
Elevation gain: 800 feet
Maps: U.S.G.S. Lake
        Trails Illustrated Yellowstone Lake

Summary of hike: The Elephant Back Loop climbs the east flank of Elephant Back Mountain at the north end of Yellowstone Lake near Fishing Bridge. The trail leads to an overlook of the expansive lake, with panoramic vistas of Stevenson Island, Dot Island, Frank Island, Pelican Valley, Lake Village, the rugged peaks of the Absaroka Mountain Range rising above the eastern shore, and the beginning of the Yellowstone River as it flows out of the lake. The trail climbs 800 feet through Engelmann spruce, lodgepole pine, and subalpine fir to the overlook.

Driving directions: From Fishing Bridge Junction, drive 1.1 miles southwest towards West Thumb to the parking area on the right.

From West Thumb, drive 19.5 miles northeast towards Fishing Bridge to the parking area on the left.

Hiking directions: From the parking area, the trail parallels the road for a short distance, then curves to the right into the lodgepole forest and begins climbing. At one mile is a trail junction, the beginning of the loop. The easier route is the trail to the left, circling in a clockwise direction. Switchbacks lead up to the summit and an overlook of Yellowstone Lake, with a bird's eye view of the enormous body of water. From the overlook, the trail loops back to the northeast. Descend along additional switchbacks and complete the loop. Return to the left, back to the parking area.

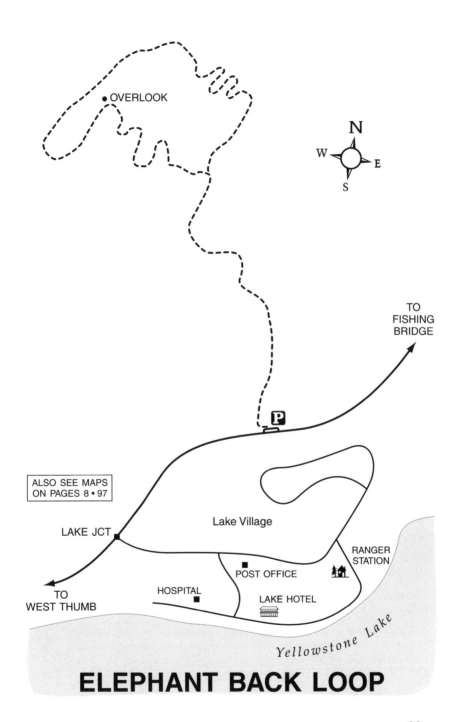

OVERLOOK

N
W   E
S

TO
FISHING
BRIDGE

P

ALSO SEE MAPS
ON PAGES 8 • 97

Lake Village

LAKE JCT

RANGER
STATION

POST OFFICE

HOSPITAL

LAKE HOTEL

TO
WEST THUMB

Yellowstone Lake

ELEPHANT BACK LOOP

Hike 44
Natural Bridge Trail

...g distance: 3 miles round trip
Hiking time: 1.5 hours
Elevation gain: Near-level
Maps: U.S.G.S. Lake
    Trails Illustrated Yellowstone Lake

Summary of hike: Natural Bridge is a 51-foot cliff with a natural 30-foot long bridge spanning a large hole in the cliff. This unique formation, sculptured by the freezing and thawing of water over centuries, is the only rock arch in Yellowstone. Bridge Creek, which carved the eroded formation, flows under the bridge beneath the formation. Two routes access the bridge—a barricaded paved road, closed to vehicles in the early 1990s, and a forested footpath. This hike follows the footpath, skirting the Bridge Bay Campground and the Bridge Bay Marina before merging with the road.

Driving directions: From Fishing Bridge Junction, drive 3.1 miles southwest towards West Thumb. Turn right at the Bridge Bay Campground entrance. In a short distance, turn left and park in the Bridge Bay Marina parking lot.

Hiking directions: Hike north, on the edge of the campground and parallel to the campground road, to the posted trailhead. Bear left into the lodgepole pine forest, and curve around the west end of the Bridge Bay Marina. Cross a bridge over an inlet stream. At 0.6 miles, the path reaches a junction with the old road. Take the road to the right, meandering through a long, narrow meadow fed by Bridge Creek. As you near the natural bridge, there is a road split that forms a loop. The right fork is the more direct route. At the bridge is an interpretive exhibit. A path follows the right of the creek and zigzags up to the top of the rock bridge. From the summit are views under the arch and through the hole. To return, complete the road loop and follow the same route to the trailhead.

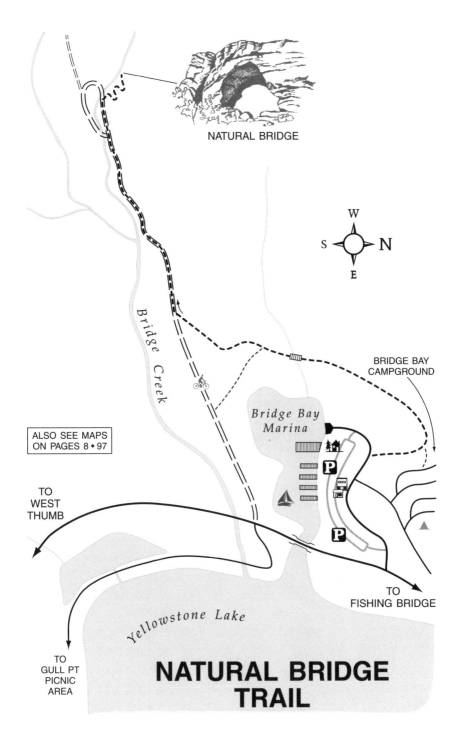

NATURAL BRIDGE

W
S N
E

BRIDGE BAY
CAMPGROUND

Bridge Creek

*Bridge Bay
Marina*

ALSO SEE MAPS
ON PAGES 8 • 97

P

P

TO
WEST
THUMB

TO
FISHING BRIDGE

Yellowstone Lake

TO
GULL PT
PICNIC
AREA

NATURAL BRIDGE
TRAIL

Hike 45
West Thumb Geyser Basin

Hiking distance: 0.7 mile loop
Hiking time: 30 minutes
Elevation gain: 50 feet
Maps: U.S.G.S. West Thumb
Trails Illustrated Yellowstone Lake
Yellowstone Association—West Thumb Geyser Basin

Summary of hike: The West Thumb Geyser Basin sits on the circular bay of West Thumb at the far west end of Yellowstone Lake. The small but diverse geyser basin is the largest basin on the shore of the lake, with a great concentration of thermal activity. A half-mile boardwalk circles the perimeter of the basin and skirts the shoreline. A quarter-mile inner loop meanders through the middle of the basin. The boardwalk passes a series of bubbling springs, which flow into the lake, and pristine, colorful pools. Highlights include Surging Spring and the electrifying blue Abyss Pool, one of the deepest pools in Yellowstone. Volcano-shaped Fishing Cone and boiling Lakeshore Geyser rise above the shallow shoreline waters of Yellowstone Lake, while Overhanging Geyser is perched over the lake to the north.

Driving directions: At West Thumb, park in the signed West Thumb Geyser Basin parking lot.

Hiking directions: From the parking lot, walk east towards the boardwalk. Just before reaching the historic log cabin ranger station, built in 1925 (now a bookstore), follow the boardwalk to a T-junction at the West Thumb Geyser Basin Loop. Sweeping views extend across Yellowstone Lake, backed by the jagged Absaroka Range. Bear right, passing Thumb Paint Pots and Bluebell Pools as the boardwalk curves downhill to the edge of Yellowstone Lake. Parallel the lakeshore, overlooking rocky beaches, eroded cliffs, and crater-like contours. Pass bubbling Lakeshore Geyser, Fishing

Cone, and Big Cone. At the west end of the loop is the clear and deep Black Pool and Abyss Pool, descending 53 feet. Complete the loop and return to the parking lot.

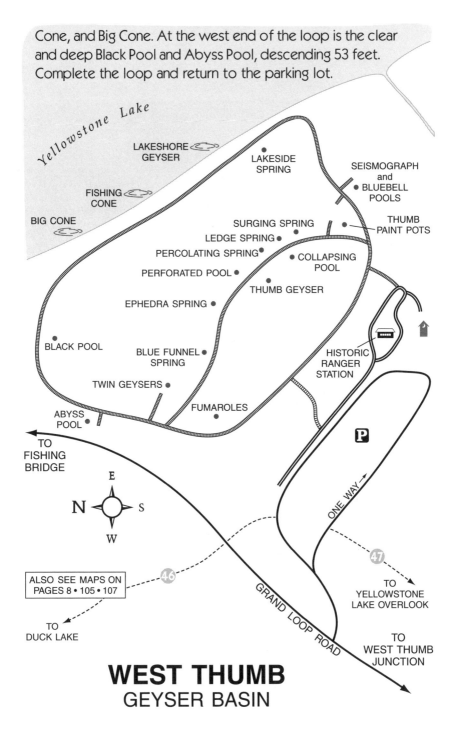

Yellowstone Lake

LAKESHORE GEYSER

LAKESIDE SPRING

SEISMOGRAPH and BLUEBELL POOLS

FISHING CONE

THUMB PAINT POTS

BIG CONE

SURGING SPRING

LEDGE SPRING

PERCOLATING SPRING

PERFORATED POOL

COLLAPSING POOL

THUMB GEYSER

EPHEDRA SPRING

BLACK POOL

BLUE FUNNEL SPRING

HISTORIC RANGER STATION

TWIN GEYSERS

FUMAROLES

ABYSS POOL

TO FISHING BRIDGE

P

E

N → ← S

W

ONE WAY →

46

47

ALSO SEE MAPS ON PAGES 8 • 105 • 107

TO DUCK LAKE

GRAND LOOP ROAD

TO YELLOWSTONE LAKE OVERLOOK

TO WEST THUMB JUNCTION

WEST THUMB
GEYSER BASIN

Hike 46
Duck Lake

Hiking distance: 1 mile round trip
Hiking time: 30 minutes
Elevation gain: 200 feet
Maps: U.S.G.S. West Thumb
Trails Illustrated Yellowstone Lake

Summary of hike: Duck Lake is a 37-acre lake that sits in a deep basin at West Thumb, between Potts Hot Spring Basin to the north and West Thumb Geyser Basin to the southeast. The round, crater-like lake is surrounded by lodgepole pine, spruce, and fir and is less than 0.2 miles from Yellowstone Lake. The half-mile trail follows a ridge between the two lakes, with scenic vistas of the Absaroka Range across Yellowstone Lake. The hike begins at the West Thumb Geyser Basin (Hike 45). This short, secluded hike to Duck Lake is a good extension to the half-mile loop around the geyser basin.

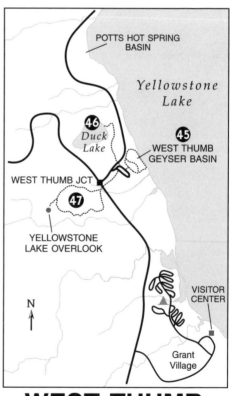

Driving directions:
At West Thumb, park in the signed West Thumb Geyser Basin parking lot.

Hiking directions:
The signed trailhead is at the north corner of the parking lot near the road to Fishing Bridge. Take the path 20 yards, and cross the road at the

WEST THUMB

crosswalk. After crossing, head north up the gentle slope through the lodgepole pine forest. Cross under power lines to a knoll overlooking Yellowstone Lake on the right and Duck Lake to the left. Follow the path on the east side of Duck Lake along the ridge separating the two bodies of water. Bear to the left and descend to the end of the trail at the lakeshore. Return along the same path.

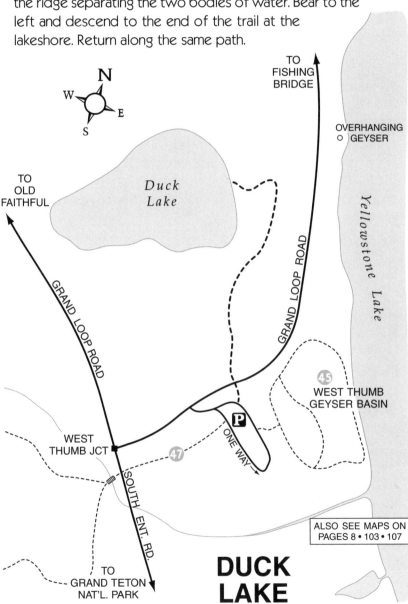

N
W E
S

TO FISHING BRIDGE

OVERHANGING GEYSER

TO OLD FAITHFUL

Duck Lake

Yellowstone Lake

GRAND LOOP ROAD

GRAND LOOP ROAD

45
WEST THUMB GEYSER BASIN

P

ONE WAY

WEST THUMB JCT

47

SOUTH ENT. RD.

ALSO SEE MAPS ON
PAGES 8 • 103 • 107

TO GRAND TETON NAT'L. PARK

DUCK LAKE

Hike 47
Yellowstone Lake Overlook

Hiking distance: 2 mile loop
Hiking time: 1 hour
Elevation gain: 230 feet
Maps: U.S.G.S. West Thumb
       Trails Illustrated Yellowstone Lake

Summary of hike: The Yellowstone Lake Overlook is an easy hike up to a knoll with commanding views of the West Thumb of Yellowstone Lake, Duck Lake (Hike 46), the West Thumb Geyser Basin (Hike 45), Mount Sheridan, and the sharp peaks of the Absaroka Range rising above the eastern shore of the lake. The trail heads through a forest and high mountain meadow to the overlook at the westernmost point of this grand body of water, encompassing 136 square miles. The Continental Divide lies just two miles to the southwest.

Driving directions: At West Thumb, park in the signed West Thumb Geyser Basin parking lot.

Hiking directions: The signed trailhead is at the southwest end of the parking lot. Walk across the grassy meadow with stands of pines. Cross the South Entrance Road, and continue through the forest to a log bridge and "Overlook" sign. Begin the loop portion of the hike by crossing the bridge to the right. Wind through the partially burned forest past dormant thermal depressions. Climb up a small rise, then cross the level ridge to a second hill. Ascend the second hill to a side path on the right. Head up the side path to the overlook with an old log bench and down trees for sitting. After enjoying the views, return to the main trail and continue to the right (south). Head through an open forest, then through a burned forest carpeted with new lodgepole pines. Return to the log bridge, completing the loop. Cross the road and return to the trailhead.

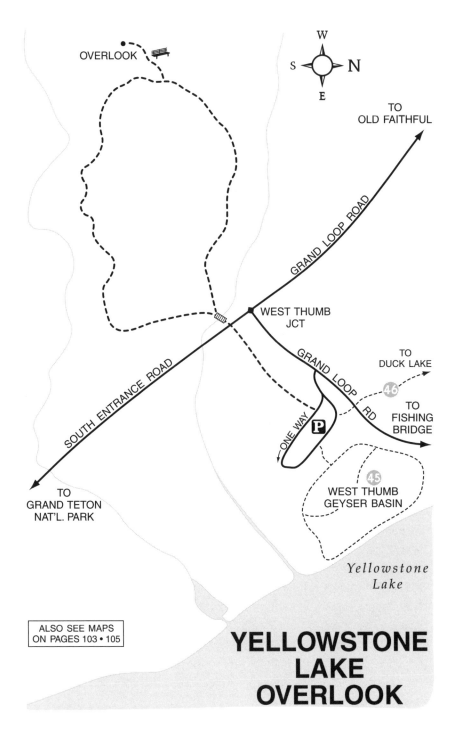

OVERLOOK

W
S ⊕ N
E

TO
OLD FAITHFUL

GRAND LOOP ROAD

WEST THUMB
JCT

GRAND LOOP RD

TO
DUCK LAKE

46

TO
FISHING
BRIDGE

ONE WAY

P

SOUTH ENTRANCE ROAD

TO
GRAND TETON
NAT'L. PARK

45

WEST THUMB
GEYSER BASIN

Yellowstone
Lake

ALSO SEE MAPS
ON PAGES 103 • 105

YELLOWSTONE
LAKE
OVERLOOK

Hike 48
Riddle Lake Trail

Hiking distance: 5 miles round trip
Hiking time: 2.5 hours
Elevation gain: Level
Maps: U.S.G.S. Mount Sheridan
       Trails Illustrated Old Faithful

Summary of hike: Riddle Lake, just south of Grant Village, sits on the east edge of the Continental Divide at an elevation of 7,913 feet. Solution Creek, the outlet stream on the east side of the 274-acre lake, drains into the West Thumb of Yellowstone Lake. Along the west end of the lake is an expansive marshland, a good habitat for moose and a wide variety of birds. The level trail is an easy hike through forests of lodgepole pines and flower-filled meadows patterned with streams. The trail skirts the edge of expansive wetlands, with Mount Sheridan and the Red Mountains providing a scenic backdrop.

This area is a bear management area. The Park Service has been closing access to the area from April 30 through mid-July. This allows the bears to pursue their natural behavior patterns without disturbance. Use caution and check with the rangers before heading to Riddle Lake.

Driving directions: From West Thumb, drive 4 miles south towards Grand Teton National Park to the trailhead parking area on the left. It is located 0.1 mile past the Continental Divide sign.

Hiking directions: From the posted trail, head east on the near-level path. Cross the Continental Divide at 0.2 miles on the ridge of the gently rolling terrain. Stroll through lodgepole forests and small, flowering meadows with streams under the shadow of the Red Mountains and Mount Sheridan to the south. The path skirts the vast marshland on the south, reaching the northwest corner of Riddle Lake at 2 miles. The path follows the northern shoreline on dry ground for a half mile to a beach, where the trail ends.

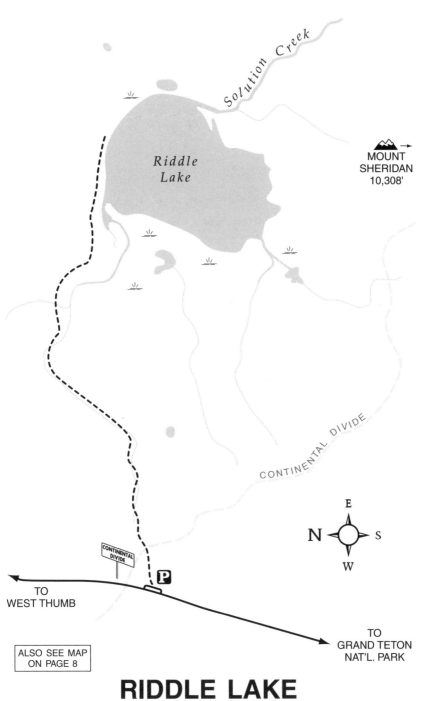

Solution Creek

Riddle Lake

MOUNT
SHERIDAN
10,308'

CONTINENTAL DIVIDE

CONTINENTAL
DIVIDE

P

TO
WEST THUMB

TO
GRAND TETON
NAT'L. PARK

E
N ✦ S
W

ALSO SEE MAP
ON PAGE 8

RIDDLE LAKE

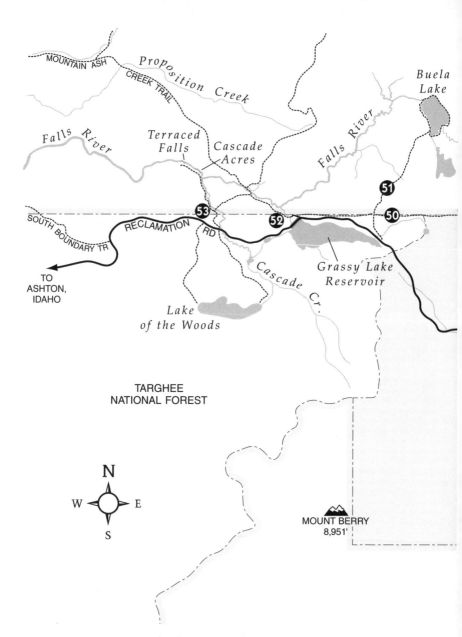

MOUNTAIN ASH

Proposition Creek

CREEK TRAIL

Falls River

Terraced Falls

Cascade Acres

Falls River

Buela Lake

53

52

51

50

SOUTH BOUNDARY TR   RECLAMATION   RD

TO
ASHTON,
IDAHO

*Grassy Lake
Reservoir*

Cascade Cr.

*Lake
of the Woods*

TARGHEE
NATIONAL FOREST

N
W ←◇→ E
S

MOUNT BERRY
8,951'

HIKES 49–57
JOHN D. ROCKEFELLER JR.
MEMORIAL PARKWAY

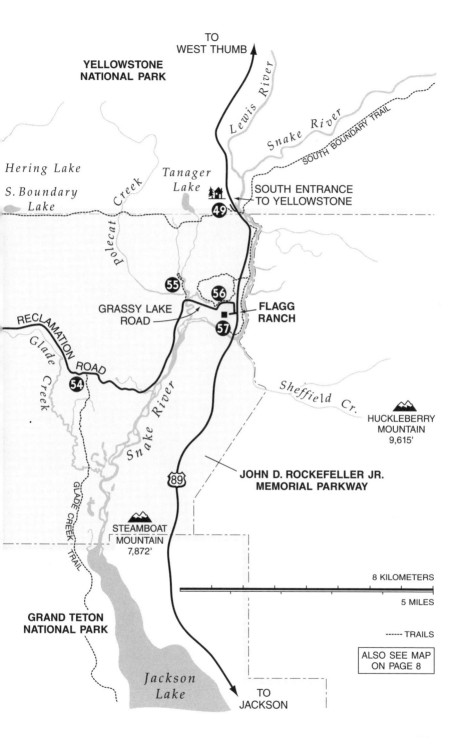

TO
WEST THUMB

**YELLOWSTONE
NATIONAL PARK**

Lewis River

Snake River

SOUTH BOUNDARY TRAIL

Hering Lake

*S. Boundary
Lake*

Polecat Creek

*Tanager
Lake*

49

SOUTH ENTRANCE
TO YELLOWSTONE

55

56

GRASSY LAKE
ROAD

**FLAGG
RANCH**

57

RECLAMATION ROAD

Glade Creek

54

Snake River

Sheffield Cr.

HUCKLEBERRY
MOUNTAIN
9,615'

GLADE CREEK TRAIL

89

JOHN D. ROCKEFELLER JR.
MEMORIAL PARKWAY

STEAMBOAT
MOUNTAIN
7,872'

8 KILOMETERS

5 MILES

------ TRAILS

ALSO SEE MAP
ON PAGE 8

**GRAND TETON
NATIONAL PARK**

*Jackson
Lake*

TO
JACKSON

Hike 49
South Boundary Lake
SOUTH BOUNDARY TRAIL from
SOUTH ENTRANCE TO YELLOWSTONE NAT'L. PARK

Hiking distance: Tanager Lake: 2 miles round trip
South Boundary Lake: 10 miles round trip
Hiking time: 1 hour to 5 hours
Elevation gain: 150 feet to 500 feet
Maps: U.S.G.S. Lewis Canyon and Grassy Lake Reservoir
Trails Illustrated Old Faithful/SW Yellowstone

*map
next page*

Summary of hike: The South Boundary Trail crosses the entire south end of Yellowstone National Park. This hike begins outside the south entrance gate of Yellowstone near the John D. Rockefeller Jr. Memorial Parkway and parallels the south boundary of the park. En route to South Boundary Lake, the trail passes Tanager Lake, a 32-acre lake in a boggy, wetland meadow. The bucolic meadow is an excellent place for spotting moose and observing birds. Three miles further west is South Boundary Lake, a forested 10-acre lake lined with pond lilies. The South Boundary Trail continues west from the lake, connecting with trails to the Pitchstone Plateau, Union Falls, and the Bechler Ranger Station. This hike can be combined with Hike 50 for a one-way, seven-mile shuttle hike.

Driving directions: From the south entrance gate of Yellowstone National Park, drive 0.2 miles south. Turn right, across the highway from the large "Leaving Yellowstone National Park" sign. Immediately pull into the parking spaces on the right.

Hiking directions: Walk up the paved service road, past the Snake River Ranger Station, to the corrals on the left. Curve around the far (north) end of the corrals to the posted trailhead. Cross the tree-dotted meadow on the faint path. Within 30 yards, the trail becomes distinct and climbs 120 feet up the hillside to the Yellowstone boundary. Follow the level tree-lined corridor west along the park boundary. At a half mile, make an easy, gradual descent through an open forest of young lodgepole pines. Curve south into the John D. Rockefeller Jr. Parkway, and cross an old log footbridge over the Tanager Lake outlet stream. Stroll through the quiet backcountry, and cross the wetland on a long wooden footbridge. Skirt the south end of the meadow, and head back into the forest. Climb an 80-foot rise, returning to the park boundary at 1.8 miles. Continue west on the level path. At 2.5 miles the trail steadily climbs through the forest to an overlook of the Snake River valley and Huckleberry Mountain in the east. The trail parallels the south edge of South Boundary Lake at 5 miles. Short side paths drop down to the shoreline. This is our turnaround spot.

The trail continues 1.5 miles to the junction with the Buela Lake Trail for a one-way, seven-mile shuttle hike with Hike 50.

Hike 50
South Boundary Lake
SOUTH BOUNDARY TRAIL from GRASSY LAKE

Hiking distance: 4.4 miles round trip
Hiking time: 2.5 hours
Elevation gain: 500 feet
Maps: U.S.G.S. Grassy Lake Reservoir and Lewis Canyon
       Trails Illustrated Old Faithful / SW Yellowstone

map
next page

Summary of hike: South Boundary Lake is an oval-shaped, 10-acre lake on the south boundary of Yellowstone National Park. The forested lake is lined with pond lilies and rimmed with lodgepole pines. Following the South Boundary Trail, the lake can be accessed from the west, near Grassy Lake, or from the east, at the south entrance to Yellowstone (Hike 49). This hike begins from Grassy Lake and climbs over a small, forested ridge to the park boundary. The trail parallels the boundary to the south edge of the lake, following the western shoreline. This hike can be combined with Hike 49 for a one-way, seven-mile shuttle hike.

Driving directions: From the south entrance gate of Yellowstone National Park, exit the park and drive 2.2 miles south to the Flagg Ranch/Grassy Lake Road turnoff at Flagg Ranch Village. Turn right and make another quick right onto Grassy Lake Road (which becomes Reclamation Road en route). Continue 9.3 miles to the unsigned Buela Lake parking pullout on the right side of the road. The pullout is a quarter mile past the large Targhee National Forest sign.

Hiking directions: Walk past the Buela Lake Trail sign, and ascend the forested ridge to an overlook of the entire 1.8-mile-

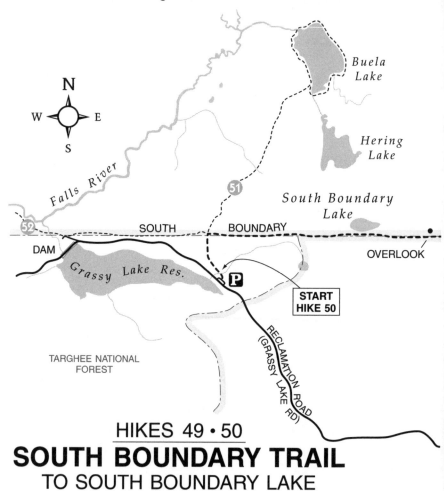

HIKES 49 • 50
SOUTH BOUNDARY TRAIL
TO SOUTH BOUNDARY LAKE

long Grassy Lake. At a half mile, atop a plateau, is a posted 4-way junction with the South Boundary Trail. The route straight ahead leads to Buela Lake (Hike 51). To the left, the South Boundary Trail leads to the Mountain Ash Creek Trail (Hike 52). Take the right fork and head east on the old access road, slowly being reclaimed by vegetation. The nearly straight path follows the south boundary of Yellowstone National Park through lodgepole pines, Englemann spruce, and subalpine fir. At 1.5 miles, the old road becomes a single track and descends into the deep forest, reaching the southwest end of South Boundary Lake at 2 miles. The trail parallels the south side of the lake, with a few short side paths dropping down to the shoreline. This is our turnaround spot.

The trail continues another 5 miles to the Snake River Ranger Station at the south entrance to Yellowstone (Hike 49).

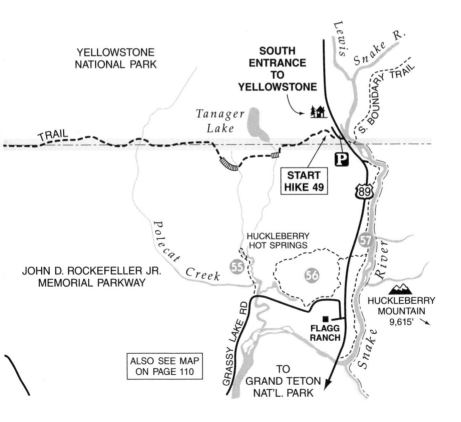

Hike 51
Buela Lake

Hiking distance: 5 miles round trip
Hiking time: 2.5 hours
Elevation gain: 400 feet
Maps: U.S.G.S. Grassy Lake Reservoir
　　　　Trails Illustrated Old Faithful/SW Yellowstone

Summary of hike: Buela Lake is a beautiful 107-acre back-country lake that sits at 7,400 feet near the south end of Yellowstone National Park. The lake is surrounded by forested hills. Yellow pond lilies grow along its marshy south end, where a stream from Hering Lake feeds the lake. The outlet stream at the northwest end of Buela Lake forms the headwaters of the Falls River. Access to the trailhead is through the John D. Rockefeller Jr. Memorial Parkway and Targhee National Forest. The well-defined trail gently winds through lodgepole pines and parallels the western shoreline past two campsites.

Driving directions: From the south entrance gate of Yellowstone National Park, exit the park and drive 2.2 miles south to the Flagg Ranch/Grassy Lake Road turnoff at Flagg Ranch Village. Turn right and make another quick right onto Grassy Lake Road (which becomes Reclamation Road en route). Continue 9.3 miles to the unsigned Buela Lake parking pullout on the right side of the road. The pullout is a quarter mile past the large Targhee National Forest sign.

Hiking directions: Walk past the trailhead sign, and ascend the hill to an overlook of the entire 1.8-mile-long Grassy Lake. At a half mile, atop a plateau, is a posted 4-way junction with the South Boundary Trail, which parallels the Yellowstone National Park boundary (Hikes 49 and 50). Continue straight ahead through a new-growth forest of lodgepole pines and aspens. Cross the gently rolling terrain, heading north inside the national park. At 2.2 miles, curve east to an overlook of Buela Lake. Descend 150 feet to the forested shoreline and a view across the lake. To the right is a swampy wetland and inlet stream from Hering Lake, a ten-minute walk to the south. The main trail curves north and follows the western shoreline past two designated campsites. Wild blueberries line the lakeside path, which circles the lake.

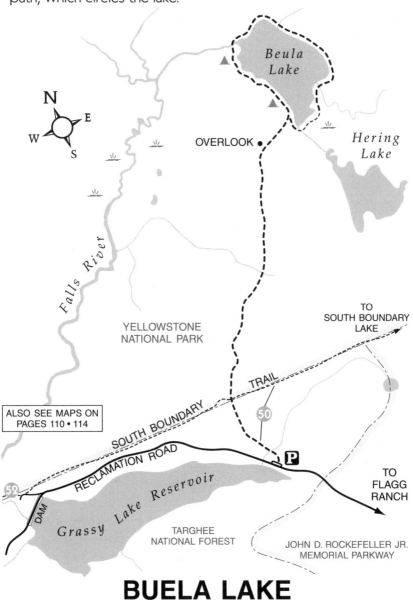

BUELA LAKE

Hike 52
Mountain Ash Creek—Cascade Creek Loop

Hiking distance: 4.3 mile loop
Hiking time: 2 hours
Elevation gain: 200 feet
Maps: U.S.G.S. Grassy Lake Reservoir
         Trails Illustrated Old Faithful/SW Yellowstone

Summary of hike: The Mountain Ash Creek Trail, on the south boundary of Yellowstone National Park, begins at the spillway below the Grassy Lake Dam. The trail leads west to Mountain Ash Creek, Union Falls, Bechler Meadows, and the Falls River Basin. This hike follows the first portion of the trail to Falls River and makes a loop back along Cascade Creek.

Driving directions: From the south entrance gate of Yellowstone National Park, exit the park and drive 2.2 miles south to the Flagg Ranch/Grassy Lake Road turnoff at Flagg Ranch Village. Turn right and make another quick right onto Grassy Lake Road (which becomes Reclamation Road en route). Continue 10.9 miles to the Grassy Lake Dam at the west end of Grassy Lake. Before crossing the dam, turn right and drive 0.2 miles downhill to the posted Mountain Ash Creek Trail and park.

Hiking directions: Cross over the spillway to the Mountain Ash Creek Trail sign. Go to the right, heading through the open forest 0.1 mile to the Yellowstone National Park boundary. Continue into the park, reaching the Falls River at a half mile. Curve left and follow the river downstream to a posted junction at 1.1 miles. The Mountain Ash Creek Trail fords Falls River and continues 6.5 miles to Union Falls. Take the South Boundary Trail to the left, skirting the southwest edge of a wetland meadow. Wind through the forest and drop down to Cascade Creek at a rock wall. Cross the creek to a junction at 2 miles. The right fork parallels Cascade Creek and Falls River to Terraced Falls (Hike 53). This hike stays to the left and ascends the hill. Steadily gain elevation, leaving Yellowstone National Park, to

Grassy Lake Road in the Targhee National Forest. Bear left on the unpaved road, crossing over Cascade Creek. Follow the road 1.6 miles to the Grassy Lake Dam. Cross the dam and bear left on the road, descending back to the trailhead.

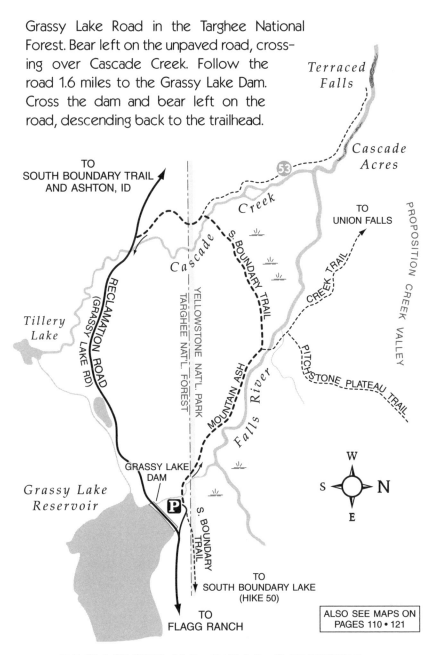

MOUNTAIN ASH CREEK– CASCADE CREEK LOOP

Hike 53
Cascade Creek Trail to Terraced Falls

Hiking distance: 3.8 miles round trip
Hiking time: 2 hours
Elevation gain: 300 feet
Maps: U.S.G.S. Grassy Lake Reservoir
        Trails Illustrated Old Faithful/SW Yellowstone

Summary of hike: Terraced Falls is a six-tiered cataract on the Falls River, plunging 140 feet between steep volcanic columns of rock. The trail to Terraced Falls also passes a series of magnificent waterfalls and powerful whitewater cascades along both Cascade Creek and Falls River. Cascade Creek is a short but stunning creek that connects Tillery Lake, just outside the national park in the Targhee National Forest, to Falls River. The trail parallels the creek past a steady series of whitewater cascades and waterfalls. Below the confluence of Cascade Creek and Falls River is Cascade Acres, a segmented set of rapids that extends 200 yards along a stretch of the creek.

Driving directions: From the south entrance gate of Yellowstone National Park, exit the park and drive 2.2 miles south to the Flagg Ranch/Grassy Lake Road turnoff at Flagg Ranch Village. Turn right and make another quick right onto Grassy Lake Road (which becomes Reclamation Road en route). Continue 10.9 miles to the Grassy Lake Dam at the west end of Grassy Lake. Cross the dam, and drive 1.7 miles to the trailhead on the right, just after crossing the bridge over Cascade Creek.

Hiking directions: Head downhill on the Cascade Creek Trail, a narrow, rocky road overlooking the Proposition Creek valley. Stay on the west side of Cascade Creek, entering Yellowstone National Park at 0.35 miles. Drop down to a posted junction at Cascade Creek. The right fork crosses the creek to Falls River (Hike 52). Bear left on the Terraced Falls Trail, and parallel Cascade Creek through an open lodgepole pine forest. Pass cascades over long slabs of rock, a rock grotto, and a series of waterfalls. At 1.2 miles, the trail reaches the confluence of Cascade Creek and Falls River at a wide, sweeping S-bend in the river. Follow the river downstream past Cascade Acres, a 200-yard cascade by large rock formations and caves. Traverse the hillside high above the river, and slowly descend to the riverbank. The trail ends at an overlook of Terraced Falls, the river, and Birch Hills.

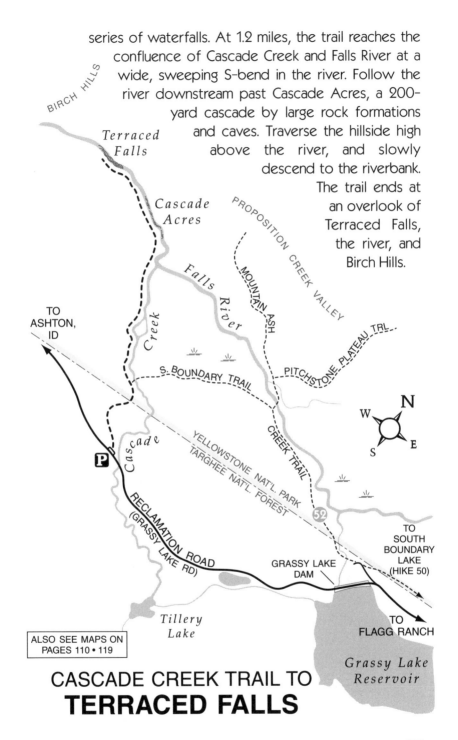

ALSO SEE MAPS ON
PAGES 110 • 119

CASCADE CREEK TRAIL TO
TERRACED FALLS

Hike 54
Glade Creek Trail
JOHN D. ROCKEFELLER JR. MEMORIAL PARKWAY

Hiking distance: 3 miles round trip
Hiking time: 1.5 hours
Elevation gain: 200 feet
Maps: U.S.G.S. Flagg Ranch
Trails Illustrated Old Faithful/SW Yellowstone

Summary of hike: Glade Creek begins just east of Grassy Lake in the undeveloped John D. Rockefeller Jr. Memorial Parkway, a 37-square-mile corridor connecting Yellowstone National Park with Grand Teton National Park. The creek flows south, joining the Snake River above Jackson Lake. The Glade Creek Trail heads into Grand Teton National Park along the west side of Jackson Lake en route to Jenny Lake. This hike follows the first 1.5 miles to Glade Creek on an easy, well-defined path. The trail heads due south through a dense conifer forest en route to a wide valley overlooking the Snake River.

Driving directions: From the south entrance gate of Yellowstone National Park, exit the park and drive 2.2 miles south to the Flagg Ranch/Grassy Lake Road turnoff at Flagg Ranch Village. Turn right and make another quick right onto Grassy Lake Road. Continue 4.4 miles to the trailhead parking area on the left.

Hiking directions: Head south through the flat, open lodgepole pine forest. Cross a wooden footbridge over a small tributary stream of Glade Creek. The path heads down a long gradual descent. At 1.2 miles, views open up of the Snake River in a wide valley. Descend to the valley floor to a log footbridge over Glade Creek. This is the turnaround spot. To return, retrace your steps.

To hike further, cross the bridge and traverse the meadow along the west edge of the marshes lining the Snake River. The trail reaches the Grand Teton National Park boundary at 3.5 miles and continues along Jackson Lake. The Glade Creek Trail connects with a series of trails leading west to Jackass Pass, Owl Creek, Berry Creek, and Webb Canyon.

GRAND TETON NAT'L. PARK

TO JACKSON LAKE

STEAMBOAT MOUNTAIN 7,437'

JOHN D. ROCKEFELLER JR. MEMORIAL PARKWAY

S

E ✦ W

N

Snake River

Glade Creek

RECLAMATION ROAD (GRASSY LAKE RD)

TO FLAGG RANCH

P

ALSO SEE MAP ON PAGE 110

GLADE CREEK TRAIL
JOHN D. ROCKEFELLER JR. PARKWAY

Hike 55
Huckleberry Hot Springs
JOHN D. ROCKEFELLER JR. MEMORIAL PARKWAY

Hiking distance: 1 mile round trip
Hiking time: 30 minutes
Elevation gain: Level
Maps: U.S.G.S. Flagg Ranch
Trails Illustrated Old Faithful/SW Yellowstone

Summary of hike: Huckleberry Hot Springs is a natural hot springs in a beautiful mountain meadow between Yellowstone and Grand Teton National Parks. The springs, in excess of 100° Fahrenheit, have a series of pools, a waterfall, a grotto, and a natural bridge. The hot springs are located along a small tributary stream of Polecat Creek, which empties into the Snake River two miles downstream. The short, easy hike is a popular cross-country ski route in the winter.

Driving directions: From the south entrance gate of Yellowstone National Park, exit the park and drive 2.2 miles south to the Flagg Ranch/Grassy Lake Road turnoff at Flagg Ranch Village. Turn right and make another quick right onto Grassy Lake Road. Continue 1.1 miles to the unmarked trailhead parking pullout on the right, located immediately after crossing the bridge over Polecat Creek.

Hiking directions: From the parking pullout, hike north past the "no bikes and no dogs" undesignated trail sign. After 100 yards the trail splits. Bear to the right and wade through the 20-foot wide Polecat Creek. Careful footing is advised as the current is stronger than it appears. After crossing, the trail leads into a meadow. Near the middle of the meadow is a stream. This is the beginning of the hot springs. Follow the stream to the left, heading upstream to a series of warm water pools. Return by retracing your steps.

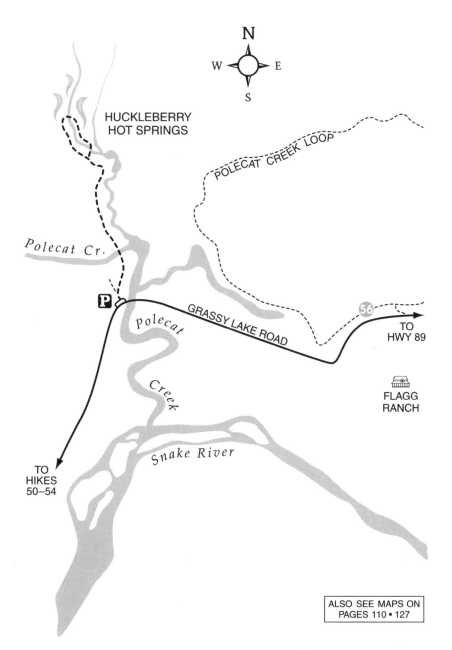

HUCKLEBERRY HOT SPRINGS
JOHN D. ROCKEFELLER JR. PARKWAY

Hike 56
Polecat Creek Loop Trail
JOHN D. ROCKEFELLER JR. MEMORIAL PARKWAY

Hiking distance: 2.3 mile loop
Hiking time: 1 hour
Elevation gain: 100 feet
Maps: U.S.G.S. Flagg Ranch
Trails Illustrated Old Faithful/SW Yellowstone

Summary of hike: Polecat Creek begins a couple of miles northwest of Yellowstone National Park's south entrance. The creek flows south, joining the Snake River west of Flagg Ranch. The Polecat Creek Loop begins at Flagg Ranch in the John D. Rockefeller Jr. Memorial Parkway. This hike is a leisurely walk with little elevation gain. The trail follows a ridge overlooking the lush marshy meadows along Polecat Creek. The wetlands are rich with waterfowl and songbirds. The trail traverses a lodgepole pine, subalpine fir, and Engelmann spruce forest.

Driving directions: From the south entrance gate of Yellowstone Park, exit the park and drive 2.2 miles south to the Flagg Ranch/Grassy Lake Road turnoff at Flagg Ranch Village. Turn right and make another quick right onto Grassy Lake Road. Park at the north end of the visitor center parking lot, across from the horse stables, on the south side of Grassy Lake Road.

Hiking directions: Walk 40 yards to the left (west) along Grassy Lake Road to the unsigned footpath on the right. The footpath connects with the signed Polecat Creek Loop 20 yards ahead. Bear left, parallel to Grassy Lake Road, hiking the loop clockwise through a lodgepole pine forest. Cross an unpaved service road and continue to the west. A short distance ahead, curve right and follow Polecat Creek above the wet, green meadow. At 1.3 miles, the path recrosses the service road to a signed junction with the Flagg Canyon Connector Trail on the left. Stay on the main trail to the right, completing the loop at Grassy Lake Road 0.5 miles ahead.

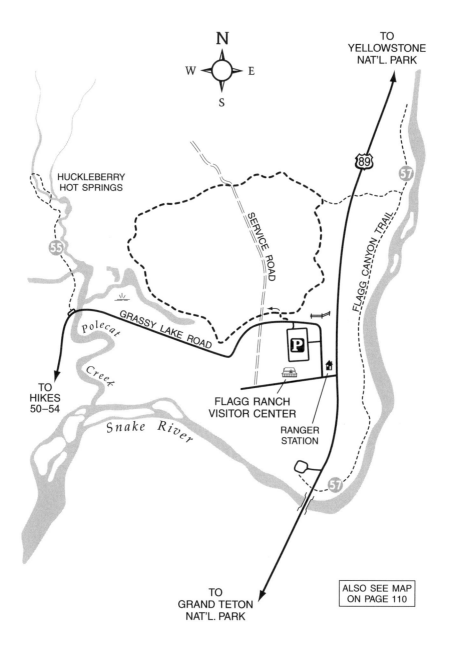

N
W · E
S

TO
YELLOWSTONE
NAT'L. PARK

HUCKLEBERRY
HOT SPRINGS

SERVICE ROAD

FLAGG CANYON TRAIL

89

57

55

GRASSY LAKE ROAD

Polecat

P

TO
HIKES
50–54

Creek

Snake River

FLAGG RANCH
VISITOR CENTER

RANGER
STATION

57

TO
GRAND TETON
NAT'L. PARK

ALSO SEE MAP
ON PAGE 110

POLECAT CREEK LOOP
JOHN D. ROCKEFELLER JR. PARKWAY

Hike 57
Flagg Canyon Trail
JOHN D. ROCKEFELLER JR. MEMORIAL PARKWAY

Hiking distance: 5 miles round trip
Hiking time: 2.5 hours
Elevation gain: 100 feet
Maps: U.S.G.S. Flagg Ranch and Lewis Canyon
      Trails Illustrated Old Faithful/SW Yellowstone

Summary of hike: The Snake River emerges from its headwaters in Yellowstone National Park, then flows through Flagg Canyon before entering Jackson Lake. This hike on the Flagg Canyon Trail follows the Snake River through the rugged, volcanic canyon along the cliff's edge.

Driving directions: From the south entrance gate of Yellowstone National Park, exit the park and drive 2.7 miles south on Highway 89 to the parking area on the west (right) side of the road. The large parking area is near the highway bridge on the north side of the Snake River. The parking area is a half mile south of the Flagg Ranch/Grassy Lake Road turnoff at Flagg Ranch Village.

Hiking directions: Cross the highway and pick up the trail along the north bank of the Snake River next to the Flagg Ranch Bridge. Follow the river upstream to the north. Climb a small hill, then follow the forested bluffs above the west bank of the river. At 0.8 miles, notice the cascades and waterfalls across the river, tumbling down the hillside tributary stream. The trail temporarily leaves the edge of the cliffs and winds through a conifer forest. At 1.2 miles, the path returns to the edge of the cliffs at a signed junction with the Polecat Creek Loop Connector Trail (Hike 56). Stay to the right, following the river past another beautiful cascade on the opposite river bank at 1.5 miles. At this point, the river narrows and swiftly flows through the steep-walled gorge of rhyolite and volcanic rock. At 2.5 miles, the trail ends at a boat launch and picnic area just south of the Yellowstone National Park boundary. Return by retracing your steps.

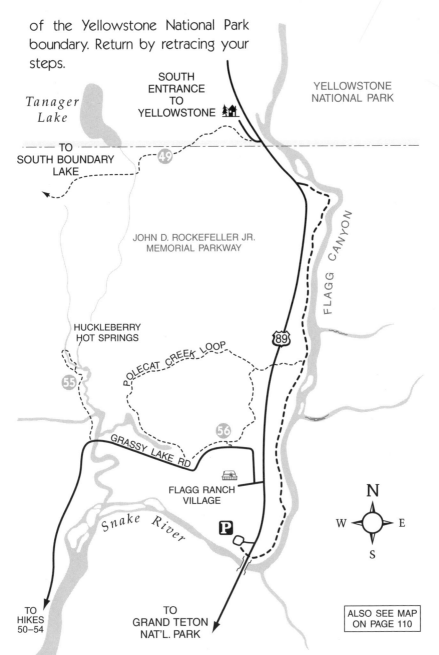

FLAGG CANYON TRAIL
JOHN D. ROCKEFELLER JR. PARKWAY

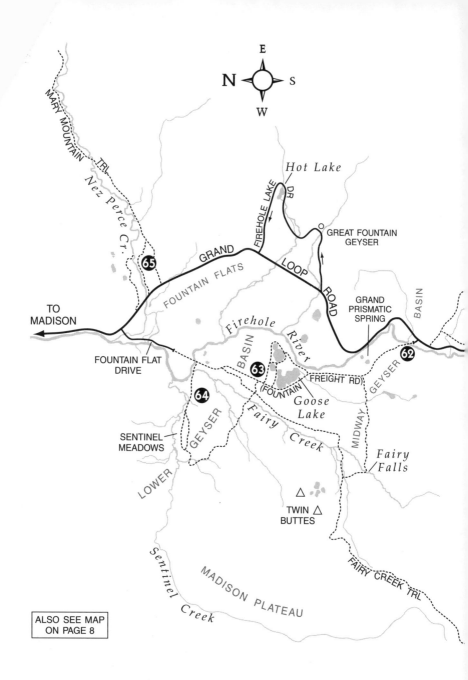

HIKES 58–65
OLD FAITHFUL AREA

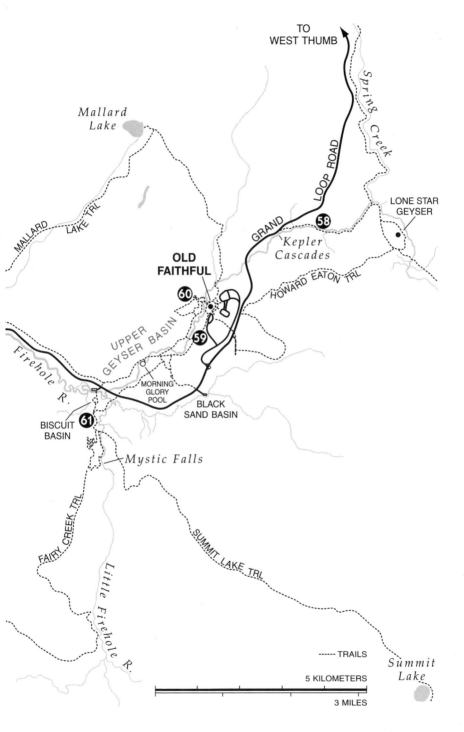

TO
WEST THUMB

Spring Creek

Mallard Lake

LONE STAR
GEYSER

MALLARD LAKE TRL

GRAND LOOP ROAD

58

Kepler Cascades

OLD FAITHFUL

HOWARD EATON TRL

60

59

UPPER GEYSER BASIN

Firehole R.

MORNING GLORY POOL

BLACK SAND BASIN

BISCUIT BASIN

61

Mystic Falls

FAIRY CREEK TRL

SUMMIT LAKE TRL

Little Firehole R.

------ TRAILS

5 KILOMETERS

3 MILES

Summit Lake

X David

Hike 58
Lone Star Geyser Trail

Hiking distance: 5 miles round trip
Hiking time: 2 hours
Elevation gain: 200 feet
Maps: U.S.G.S. Old Faithful
       Trails Illustrated Old Faithful

Summary of hike: Lone Star Geyser, an isolated 12-foot geyserite cone, is one of Yellowstone's largest cones. The geyser erupts in predictable three-hour intervals, shooting 30- to 50-feet high for a full 30 minutes. The easy, near-level trail parallels the upper Firehole River through a beautiful river valley the entire way to Lone Star Geyser. There are never large crowds in this undeveloped natural area. The impressive eruption is a memorable backcountry experience and an event that is well worth the wait.

Driving directions: From Old Faithful, take the main road south towards West Thumb 3.7 miles to the Lone Star Geyser parking area. It is located just past the well-marked Kepler Cascades on the right.

    From West Thumb, drive 13 miles west to the Lone Star Geyser parking area on the left, just before Kepler Cascades.

Hiking directions: Head south on the posted trail, an old road used to access the Lone Star Geyser before 1972. The level road parallels the east bank of the Firehole River through a beautiful forest of lodgepole pine, Engelmann spruce, and Douglas fir. At 0.6 miles, cross a concrete bridge over the river, and leisurely stroll upstream on the river's west bank. At 1.6 miles, pass a junction with the Spring Creek Trail, an old stage-coach route at the mouth of Spring Creek. As the Firehole River curves away, the trail winds through a large grassy meadow. The trail reaches Lone Star Geyser a short distance ahead. Small footbridges cross over the geyser's runoff channels. After experiencing the eruption, return on the same trail.

Back at the parking lot, take a short side trip 50 yards north to Kepler Cascades, where the Firehole River dramatically drops 125 feet in a narrow gorge.

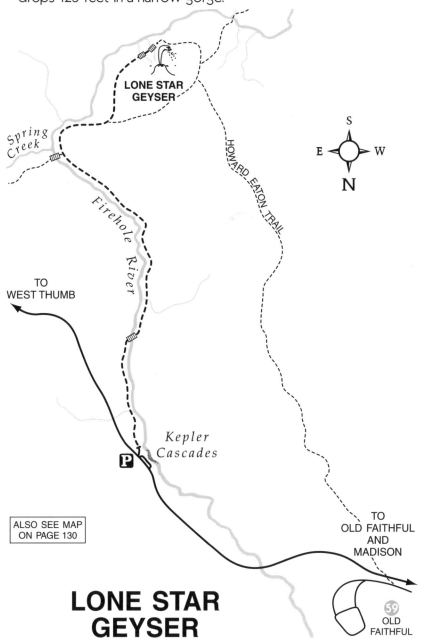

LONE STAR GEYSER

Spring Creek

Firehole River

HOWARD EATON TRAIL

S

E ⊕ W

N

TO WEST THUMB

Kepler Cascades

P

ALSO SEE MAP ON PAGE 130

TO OLD FAITHFUL AND MADISON

59 OLD FAITHFUL

LONE STAR GEYSER

Hike 59
Upper Geyser Basin
THE BOARDWALKS AT OLD FAITHFUL

Hiking distance: 2 to 4 miles round trip
Hiking time: 1 to 3 hours
Elevation gain: Level
Maps: U.S.G.S. Old Faithful
Trails Illustrated Old Faithful
Yellowstone Association—Old Faithful Area Trail Guide

Summary of hike: The Upper Geyser Basin contains twenty percent of the world's geysers, the largest concentration on earth. The one-square-mile basin has several groups of hot springs and over 150 geysers, including Old Faithful, the most famous geyser in the world. The Firehole River flows through this half-mile-wide basin, surrounded by groups of spectacular geothermal features. Several groups of geysers are threaded together by boardwalks, walkways, and trails that loop through the basin along both sides of the Firehole River. The route passes endless rainbow-colored pools and hot springs; gurgling, bubbling, and steaming fumaroles; odd-shaped cones; and fountain-type geysers. All are in continuous motion. The predicted times of many of the eruptions are posted in the visitor center.

For a sweeping vista of the entire Upper Geyser Basin, take the trail to Observation Point (Hike 60).

Driving directions: Old Faithful is 16.3 miles south of Madison and 17 miles west of West Thumb. Exit the main road into the Old Faithful parking complex. This hike begins near the Old Faithful visitor center.

Hiking directions: From the parking lot or visitor center, walk towards Old Faithful Geyser. The boardwalks and paved trails lead throughout the geyser basin along various interconnecting loops. Whichever direction you decide to take, you will feel you chose the right route.

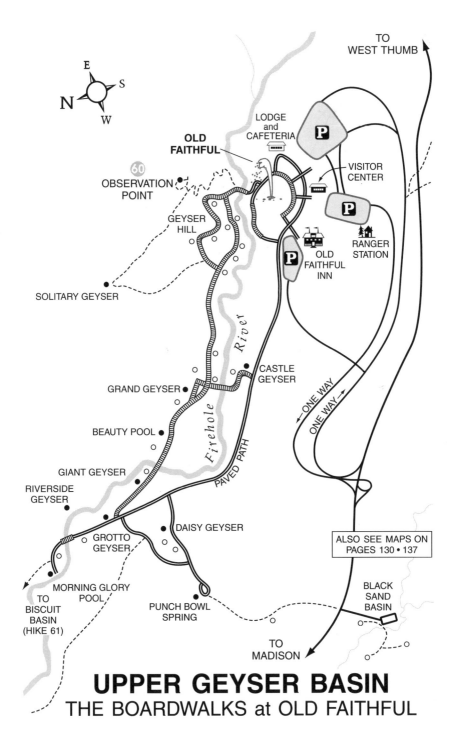

TO
WEST THUMB

E
N   S
W

LODGE
and
CAFETERIA

**OLD
FAITHFUL**

P

VISITOR
CENTER

60
OBSERVATION
POINT

P

GEYSER
HILL

P

OLD
FAITHFUL
INN

RANGER
STATION

SOLITARY GEYSER

River

Firehole

CASTLE
GEYSER

ONE WAY

ONE WAY

GRAND GEYSER

BEAUTY POOL

GIANT GEYSER

PAVED PATH

RIVERSIDE
GEYSER

ALSO SEE MAPS ON
PAGES 130 • 137

GROTTO
GEYSER

DAISY GEYSER

TO
BISCUIT
BASIN
(HIKE 61)

MORNING GLORY
POOL

PUNCH BOWL
SPRING

BLACK
SAND
BASIN

TO
MADISON

UPPER GEYSER BASIN
THE BOARDWALKS at OLD FAITHFUL

Hike 60
Observation Point Loop
UPPER GEYSER BASIN

Hiking distance: 2 mile loop
Hiking time: 1 hour
Elevation gain: 200 feet
Maps: U.S.G.S. Old Faithful
       Trails Illustrated Old Faithful
       Yellowstone Association—Old Faithful Area Trail Guide

Summary of hike: The trail to Observation Point begins at Old Faithful in the Upper Geyser Basin. The trail crosses a bridge over the Firehole River and climbs to a magnificent overlook on a rhyolitic rock outcropping. Perched on the edge of the hill, the vistas extend across the entire Upper Geyser Basin and surrounding mountains, including a bird's-eye view of Old Faithful. The loop trail descends through a lush forest to Solitary Geyser, with a 4-foot eruption every 5 to 7 minutes.

To witness the eruption of Old Faithful from the overlook, check at the visitor center for the estimated eruption time and allow 30 minutes to reach Observation Point.

Driving directions: Same as Hike 59.

Hiking directions: From the Upper Geyser Basin boardwalk between Old Faithful and the visitor center, walk east (right) towards the Old Faithful Lodge and cafeteria. Loop around the east end of the boardwalk, circling Old Faithful to a posted junction. Bear right and cross a log bridge over the Firehole River to a junction with the Observation Point Trail. Leave the boardwalk and begin the loop on the unpaved footpath to the right. Gradually wind up the forested slope to a trail fork. The left fork is the return route. Go to the right on a looping spur trail to Observation Point. The trail circles the point, with rock steps leading to the overlook and the tree-stump seats. After marveling at the views, return to the main trail, and bear right through the shady forest to Solitary Geyser. Curve sharply to the left and continue downhill, returning to the Upper Geyser Basin boardwalk and a T-junction. The shorter return route bears left back to Old Faithful and the visitor center. To continue exploring the Upper Geyser Basin, go to the right (Hike 59).

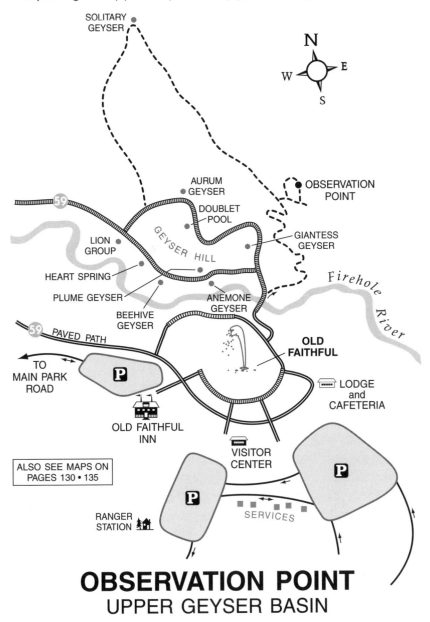

OBSERVATION POINT
UPPER GEYSER BASIN

Hike 61
Mystic Falls Loop
BISCUIT BASIN

Hiking distance: 3 miles round trip
Hiking time: 1.5 hours
Elevation gain: 800 feet
Maps: U.S.G.S. Old Faithful
Trails Illustrated Old Faithful

Summary of hike: Mystic Falls is a full-bodied, multi-tiered waterfall on the Little Firehole River. The 70-foot cataract plunges down a series of steps from the Madison Plateau to Biscuit Basin. The trail begins in Biscuit Basin, passing thermal pools and geysers on a circular wooden boardwalk. Most people visit this area specifically to view these thermal features, including Sapphire Pool and Jewel Geyser. The trail soon leaves the populated area and follows the Little Firehole River through the backcountry to Mystic Falls and an overlook of Biscuit Basin, Black Sand Basin, and the Upper Geyser Basin at Old Faithful.

Driving directions: From Old Faithful, drive north 2.5 miles to the Biscuit Basin parking area. Turn left and park.
From Madison, drive south 13.8 miles to the Biscuit Basin parking area and turn right.

Hiking directions: Cross the bridge over the Firehole River, entering Biscuit Basin. Walk to the far end of the wooden boardwalk past pools and geysers to the signed Mystic Falls Trail by Avoca Spring. Head west on the trail. At the first junction, take the lower trail to the left, beginning the loop. The lower trail parallels the Little Firehole River through lodgepole pines. Pass the Summit Lake Trail on the left, and continue upstream to Mystic Falls. Short side paths descend to the river's edge below the falls. The main trail climbs up switchbacks to the top of the falls and a ridge. Follow the ridge along the face of the Madison Plateau, passing the Fairy Creek Trail on the left. Stay to the right and loop back through lodgepole pines to an

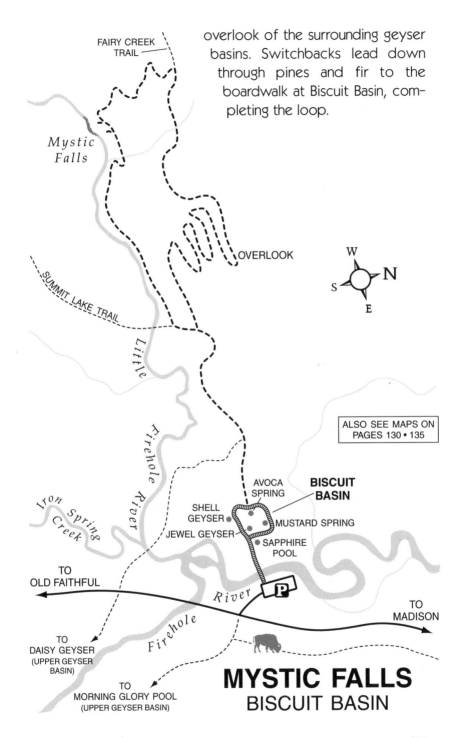

overlook of the surrounding geyser basins. Switchbacks lead down through pines and fir to the boardwalk at Biscuit Basin, completing the loop.

FAIRY CREEK TRAIL

Mystic Falls

SUMMIT LAKE TRAIL

Little

Firehole River

OVERLOOK

W
N
S
E

ALSO SEE MAPS ON
PAGES 130 • 135

Iron Spring Creek

AVOCA SPRING

BISCUIT BASIN

SHELL GEYSER

JEWEL GEYSER

MUSTARD SPRING

SAPPHIRE POOL

TO
OLD FAITHFUL

River

P

TO
MADISON

Firehole

TO
DAISY GEYSER
(UPPER GEYSER BASIN)

TO
MORNING GLORY POOL
(UPPER GEYSER BASIN)

MYSTIC FALLS
BISCUIT BASIN

X David

Hike 62
Fairy Falls

Hiking distance: 5.2 miles round trip
Hiking time: 2.5 hours
Elevation gain: Near level
Maps: U.S.G.S. Lower Geyser Basin
Trails Illustrated Old Faithful

Summary of hike: Fairy Falls is a 197-foot ribbon of water that gracefully free-falls from the Madison Plateau to the Midway Geyser Basin. The thin, delicate braids of Fairy Creek spill down the vertical rock wall into a beautiful pool in a rock grotto. The near-level hike skirts the edge of the Midway Geyser Basin parallel to the Firehole River. The trail passes geysers and hot springs, including the multi-colored Grand Prismatic Spring, the largest hot spring in North America, with a diameter of 370 feet. The path winds through a lodgepole pine forest burned in the North Fork Fire of 1988. A new regeneration of trees carpets the valley floor.

Driving directions: From Old Faithful, drive 4.6 miles north to the signed Fairy Falls turnoff on the left. Turn left and park 0.1 mile ahead in the parking lot.

From Madison, drive 11.5 miles south to the signed Fairy Falls turnoff on the right.

Hiking directions: Cross the steel bridge over the Firehole River, and head northwest along the wide Fountain Freight Road, an old wagon road built in 1883. The path parallels the Firehole River at the edge of the Madison Plateau along the Midway Geyser Basin, passing the enormous and colorful Grand Prismatic Spring and Excelsior Geyser Crater. At one mile is a signed junction with the Fairy Falls Trail. The road continues north to Goose Lake (Hike 63). Bear left on the footpath and head west, following the base of the Madison Plateau. Walk across the gentle terrain and through the burn area, arriving at the base of Fairy Falls at Fairy Creek. After enjoying the falls and pool, return to the trailhead along the same route.

To extend the hike, the trail continues 0.7 miles beyond Fairy Falls to Imperial Geyser at the base of Twin Buttes.

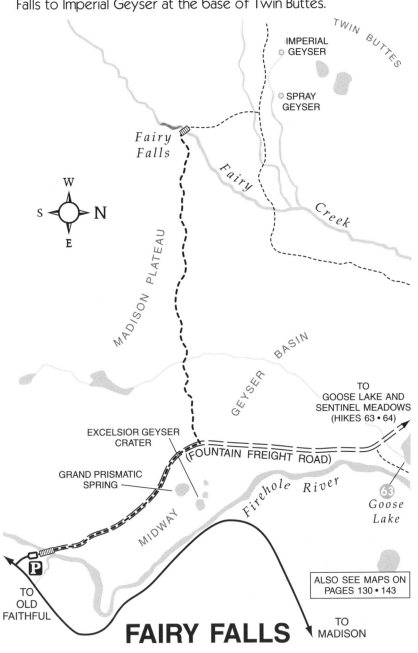

FAIRY FALLS

Hike 63
Goose Lake and Feather Lake

Hiking distance: 5.2 miles round trip
Hiking time: 2.5 hours
Elevation gain: Near level
Maps: U.S.G.S. Lower Geyser Basin
       Trails Illustrated Old Faithful

Summary of hike: Goose Lake and Feather Lake sit in a natural depression formed by volcanic and thermal activity. The lakes lie alongside the Firehole River, adjacent to Fountain Flats and the Lower Geyser Basin. This hike crosses the plateau through the Lower Geyser Basin in a beautiful meadow with hot springs and thermal mounds. The lakeside area is surrounded by lodgepole pines and is equipped with picnic facilities.

Driving directions: From Old Faithful, drive 10.5 miles north to Fountain Flat Drive on the left. Turn left and drive 0.8 miles to the trailhead parking lot at the end of the road.

From Madison, drive 5.6 miles south to Fountain Flat Drive on the right.

Hiking directions: Head south on Fountain Flat Drive, an old graveled road (originally known as Fountain Freight Road) which is closed to vehicles. Follow the road past Ojo Caliente Spring, a hot spring on the right, and cross the bridge over the Firehole River at 0.4 miles. The trail to Sentinel Meadows heads west (Hike 64). Continue straight ahead along the wide level trail, reaching Goose Lake at 1.7 miles. Stay on Fountain Flat Drive along the southwest side of Goose Lake to a junction at 2.2 miles. The trail straight ahead to the south leads to Fairy Falls (Hike 62). Bear left and follow the Firehole River less than a half mile downstream through the grassy meadow to a picnic area at Feather Lake. You can easily hike around either lake through the flat meadow. At the north end of the lakes is a circular pond. Complete your own loop back to Fountain Flat Drive. Head back along the old road to the parking area.

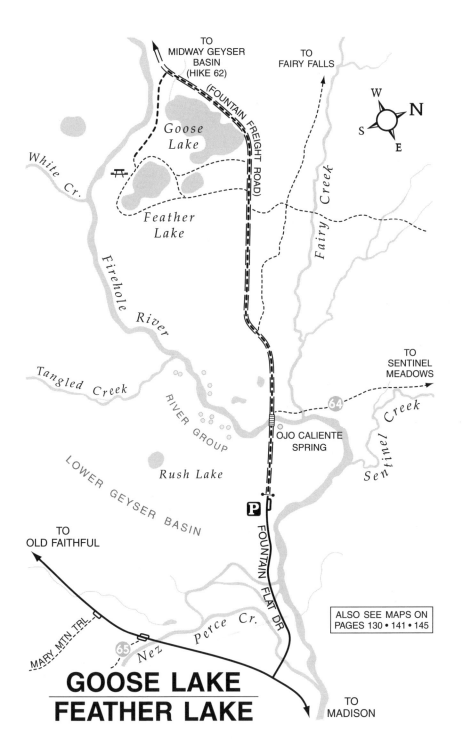

TO
MIDWAY GEYSER
BASIN
(HIKE 62)

TO
FAIRY FALLS

(FOUNTAIN FREIGHT ROAD)

N
W
S
E

*Goose
Lake*

White Cr.

*Feather
Lake*

Firehole River

Fairy Creek

Tangled Creek

RIVER GROUP

TO
SENTINEL
MEADOWS

64

Sentinel Creek

OJO CALIENTE
SPRING

Rush Lake

LOWER GEYSER BASIN

P

FOUNTAIN FLAT DR

TO
OLD FAITHFUL

MARY MTN TRL

65

Nez Perce Cr.

ALSO SEE MAPS ON
PAGES 130 • 141 • 145

TO
MADISON

GOOSE LAKE
FEATHER LAKE

Hike 64
Sentinel Meadows

Hiking distance: 3.8 miles round trip
Hiking time: 2 hours
Elevation gain: Near level
Maps: U.S.G.S. Lower Geyser Basin
       Trails Illustrated Old Faithful

Summary of hike: The hike through Sentinel Meadows leads to Queens Laundry, a small thermal area also known as Red Terrace Spring. In the 1880s, the spring was used as a bathing area. A log bath house was built, and the decaying structure still remains. Sentinel Creek, a tributary of the Firehole River, flows through the meadow. This hike crosses the Firehole River and passes numerous hot spring mounds through a flat, wet, open valley in the Lower Geyser Basin.

Driving directions: Same as Hike 63.

Hiking directions: Head south on Fountain Flat Drive, a gravel road closed to vehicles. Follow the road past Ojo Caliente Spring, a hot spring on the right along the Firehole River. Cross the bridge over the river to a signed trail on the right at 0.4 miles. Bear right, heading downstream through the meadow. Cross a footbridge over Fairy Creek. Continue through a burned area from the 1988 fires, then descend into an open meadow with stands of lodgepole pines. Cross a log bridge over a meandering stream. The trail becomes faint near an orange trail junction sign on a tree. Straight ahead, through Sentinel Meadow, are hot thermal mounds. This route can be wet and marshy in spots. If so, take the left route towards campsite OG2, leading up a knoll. This trail follows the south edge of Sentinel Meadows along the hillside. At the west end of the meadow is Queens Laundry. After exploring the area, return along the same trail. The trail also loops back southeast to Fountain Flat Drive, but the trail is difficult to follow and not recommended.

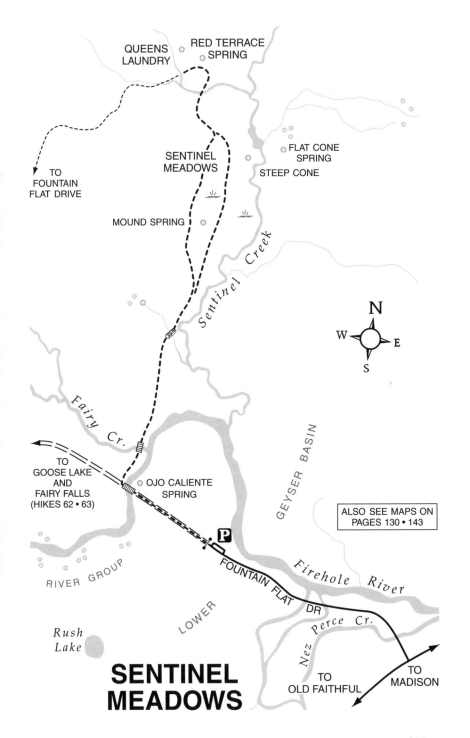

QUEENS
LAUNDRY

RED TERRACE
SPRING

TO
FOUNTAIN
FLAT DRIVE

SENTINEL
MEADOWS

FLAT CONE
SPRING

STEEP CONE

MOUND SPRING

Sentinel Creek

N
W   E
S

Fairy Cr.

TO
GOOSE LAKE
AND
FAIRY FALLS
(HIKES 62 • 63)

OJO CALIENTE
SPRING

GEYSER BASIN

ALSO SEE MAPS ON
PAGES 130 • 143

P

Firehole River

FOUNTAIN FLAT DR

RIVER GROUP

LOWER

Nez Perce Cr.

Rush
Lake

TO
OLD FAITHFUL

TO
MADISON

SENTINEL
MEADOWS

Hike 65
Nez Perce Creek

Hiking distance: 4 miles round trip
Hiking time: 2 hours
Elevation gain: Near level
Maps: U.S.G.S. Lower Geyser Basin
Trails Illustrated Old Faithful

Summary of hike: This hike parallels Nez Perce Creek, the largest tributary stream of the Firehole River, as it flows from Mary Lake through Culex Basin. The basin lies in a beautiful valley fringed with lodgepole pines. The area is home to an isolated group of hot springs, thermal pools, sinter mounds, a few geysers, and Morning Mist Springs. This trail begins across the road from Fountain Flats and the Lower Geyser Basin near the Firehole River. The hike follows the Mary Mountain Trail, an old road closed in the 1970s, and parallels Nez Perce Creek upstream for two miles to a bridge crossing.

Driving directions: From Old Faithful, drive 9.9 miles north to the paved parking pullouts on either side of the road south of Nez Perce Creek.

From Madison, drive 6.2 miles south to the paved parking pullouts after crossing Nez Perce Creek.

Hiking directions: Head east on the footpath along the south edge of Nez Perce Creek past the forested, pyramid-shaped Porcupine Hills. Along the winding creek are thermal areas and hot springs. In a half mile on the right is Morning Mist Springs, a group of thermal springs and hot clear pools. As the trail fades away, cross the meadow while exploring the various pools, then join the Mary Mountain Trail. (The Mary Mountain Trail begins at the park road in the signed parking area 0.3 miles south of Nez Perce Creek.) Bear left, heading northeast up the valley. The trail parallels the creek past a continuous series of boiling pots, hot springs, and clear pools. At two miles the road ends at a wooden footbridge crossing Nez Perce Creek. This is our turnaround spot.

To hike further, the trail continues up the valley on the north side of the creek. The path reaches Mary Lake near the summit of Mary Mountain, nine miles further.

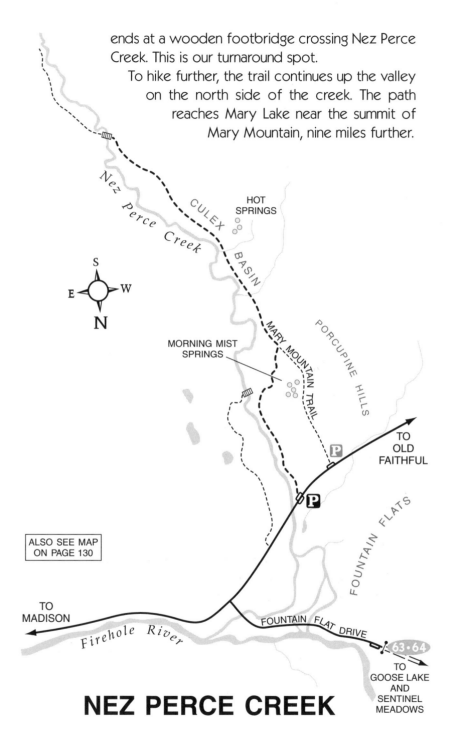

Nez Perce Creek

CULEX BASIN

HOT SPRINGS

S
W
E
N

PORCUPINE HILLS

MORNING MIST SPRINGS

MARY MOUNTAIN TRAIL

P

TO OLD FAITHFUL

P

FOUNTAIN FLATS

ALSO SEE MAP ON PAGE 130

TO MADISON

Firehole River

FOUNTAIN FLAT DRIVE

63•64

TO GOOSE LAKE AND SENTINEL MEADOWS

NEZ PERCE CREEK

Hike 66
Monument Geyser Basin Trail

Hiking distance: 3 miles round trip
Hiking time: 1.5 hours
Elevation gain: 700 feet
Maps: U.S.G.S. Norris Junction and Madison Junction
Trails Illustrated Mammoth Hot Springs

Summary of hike: Monument Geyser Basin sits on a hill 700 feet above Gibbon Canyon and Gibbon Meadows. The isolated thermal area is long and narrow with mud pots; fumaroles (steam vents); boiling sulfur caldrons; dormant, strange looking sinter cones; and Monument Geyser (also known as Thermos Bottle), a 10-foot hissing cylindrical cone. The hike follows the Gibbon River for a half mile before ascending a hill on the south edge of Gibbon Meadows. The exceptional mountaintop views from the desolate geyser basin include Gibbon Meadows, Gibbon Canyon, Mount Holmes, the Gallatin Range, and the Washburn Range. The lightly used trail up to Monument Geyser Basin allows for private tranquility in the wilderness.

Driving directions: The Monument Geyser Basin turnout is located 8.6 miles northeast from Madison and 4.7 miles southwest from Norris. The turnout is on the west side of the road just south of the bridge crossing the Gibbon River. A small sign reads "Monument" at the turnout.

Hiking directions: From the parking turnout, walk upstream along the west side of the Gibbon River. After a half mile, the trail curves west, away from the river. Climb steadily uphill through the lodgepole forest, gaining 650 feet in a half mile. The area was burned in the Yellowstone fires of 1988. A new forest of healthy lodgepole pines now covers the ground. At the top of the hill, veer to the right a short distance to this unique area. After exploring the strange-shaped formations, return along the same trail.

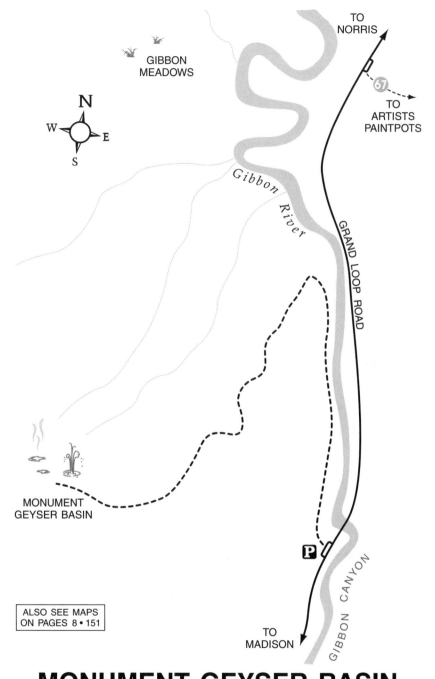

TO
NORRIS

GIBBON
MEADOWS

TO
ARTISTS
PAINTPOTS

N
W E
S

Gibbon River

GRAND LOOP ROAD

MONUMENT
GEYSER BASIN

P

ALSO SEE MAPS
ON PAGES 8 • 151

GIBBON CANYON

TO
MADISON

MONUMENT GEYSER BASIN

Hike 67
Artists Paintpots Trail

Hiking distance: 1.2 miles round trip
Hiking time: 40 minutes
Elevation gain: 100 feet
Maps: U.S.G.S. Norris Junction
       Trails Illustrated Mammoth Hot Springs

Summary of hike: The Artists Paintpots lie in the Gibbon Geyser Basin at the south end of Gibbon Meadows. This thermal group includes a variety of fumaroles (steam vents); hypnotizing, boiling mud pots; and multi-colored hot springs and pools with a spectrum of greens, reds, blues, oranges, and browns. The trail begins on a boardwalk through a wetland and passes through a colorful thermal basin at the foot of Paintpot Hill. The trail loops up and around Paintpot Hill to a series of bubbling mud pots and fumaroles. The expansive views from the hillside include the Artists Paintpots, Gibbon Meadows, Mount Holmes, Dome Mountain, and the Gallatin Range.

Driving directions: The Artists Paintpots parking area is located 9.3 miles northeast from Madison and 4 miles southwest from Norris. The turnout is on the east side of the road at the south edge of Gibbon Meadows.

Hiking directions: From the parking turnout, follow the boardwalk east through the marshy wetland along the base of a burned hillside from the 1988 fires. The level trail leads through the colorful thermal area to a junction, beginning the loop. Stay to the left in the basin, then climb up Paintpot Hill to the south. From the hillside is a vista of the colorful thermal features, Gibbon Meadows, and the surrounding mountains. The trail loops back along the hill while overlooking the area below. From the large boiling mud pot, the trail descends to the right and back to the basin bottom, completing the loop. Return along the same trail.

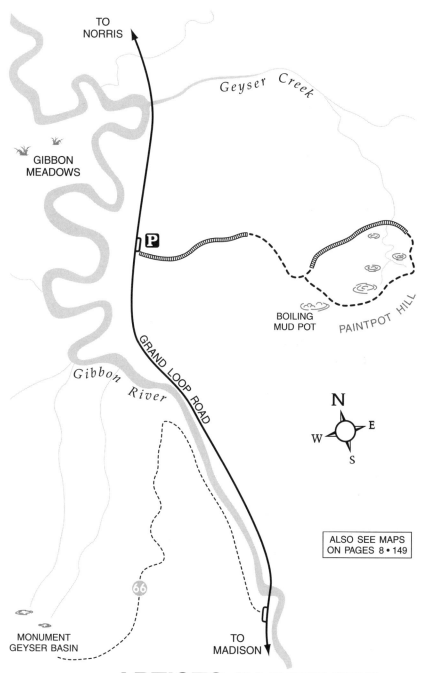

TO
NORRIS

Geyser Creek

GIBBON
MEADOWS

P

BOILING
MUD POT

PAINTPOT HILL

GRAND LOOP ROAD

Gibbon River

N
W E
S

ALSO SEE MAPS
ON PAGES 8 • 149

66

MONUMENT
GEYSER BASIN

TO
MADISON

ARTISTS PAINTPOTS

Hike 68
Harlequin Lake Trail

Hiking distance: 1 mile round trip
Hiking time: 30 minutes
Elevation gain: 120 feet
Maps: U.S.G.S. Mount Jackson
Trails Illustrated Old Faithful

Summary of hike: Harlequin Lake is a secluded 10-acre circular lake tucked at the southern base of Purple Mountain. The lake sits in a natural setting at an elevation of 6,892 feet, just west of the headwaters of the Madison River (where the Gibbon and Firehole Rivers merge). The trail to the lake is a short, easy hike through the forest. The lake is half covered in yellow water lilies and plays host to a variety of birds, but the lake does not have fish. The Yellowstone fires of 1988 burned the lodgepole pines surrounding this trail, but thousands of new-growth lodgepole pines cover the hillside (back cover photo).

Driving directions: From the West Yellowstone park entrance, drive east 11.9 miles and turn right into the parking area on the south side of the road. On the north side of the highway is a trailhead sign for Harlequin Lake.

From Madison, drive west 1.6 miles and turn left into the parking area.

Hiking directions: Cross the highway to the signed Harlequin Lake trailhead. The trail gently climbs around the hill, curving to the left. Tucked in on the other side of the hill is Harlequin Lake, surrounded by forest. The trail follows the south side of the lake, then fades out on the steep hillside to the north. Return on the same trail.

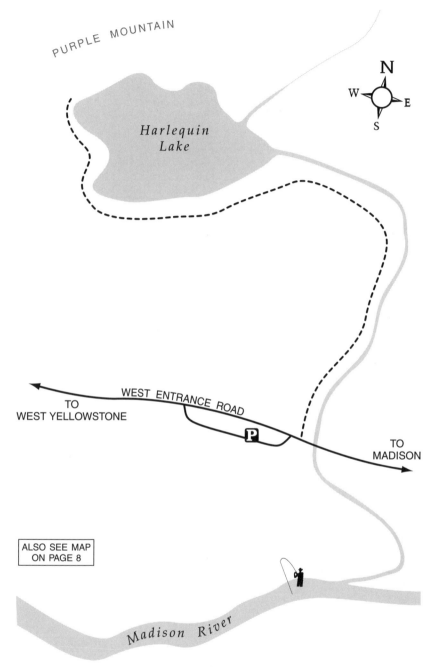

PURPLE MOUNTAIN

Harlequin Lake

N
W · E
S

WEST ENTRANCE ROAD

TO
WEST YELLOWSTONE

P

TO
MADISON

ALSO SEE MAP
ON PAGE 8

Madison River

HARLEQUIN LAKE

Hike 69
Gneiss Creek Trail
from the Madison River

Hiking distance: 2.8 miles round trip
Hiking time: 1.5 hours
Elevation gain: 150 feet
Maps: U.S.G.S. Mount Jackson
Trails Illustrated Mammoth Hot Springs

Summary of hike: The Gneiss Creek Trail is a 14-mile trail through the Madison Valley, connecting the Madison Canyon with the Gallatin to the north. This hike follows the first section of the trail starting from the southern trailhead at the Madison River, where the Madison Canyon soon opens to the expansive valley. The trail continues to the northern trailhead (Hike 78) for extended hiking. Watch for trumpeter swans, which nest on the river banks.

Driving directions: From the West Yellowstone park entrance, drive 7.3 miles east to the signed Gneiss Creek Trail on the left, just after crossing the Madison River bridge.

From Madison, drive 6.2 miles west to the trailhead parking lot on the right, just before crossing the Madison River bridge.

Hiking directions: Walk northwest along the north shore of the Madison River, heading downstream. The path hugs the edge of the steep forested cliffs along the river bank. There are frequent rises, dips, and deadfall trees. At 0.8 miles, the trail curves right, away from the Madison River, and climbs a hill to a ridge. Head north through the burned Douglas fir and lodgepole pine forest. At 1.4 miles is a signed junction with the Cougar Creek Trail. This is the turnaround spot for a 2.8-mile round-trip hike.

To hike further, the Cougar Creek Trail bears right, heading northeast to a patrol cabin on the creek. The Gneiss Creek Trail continues to the left, skirting the east edge of the Madison Valley to the northern trailhead 12.5 miles ahead (Hike 78).

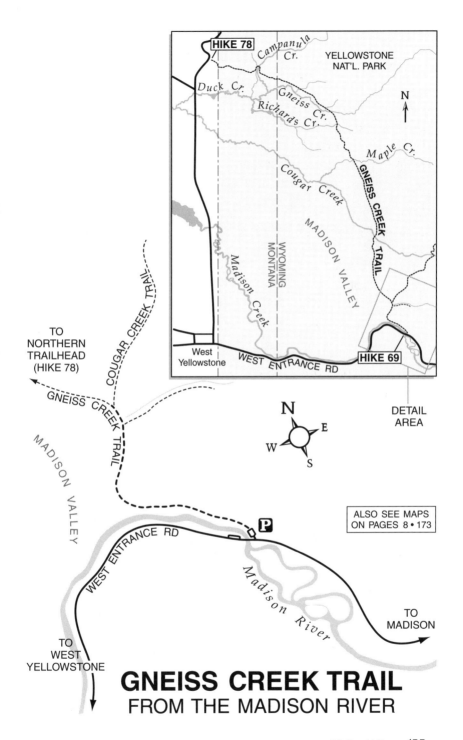

HIKE 78

Campanula Cr.

YELLOWSTONE NAT'L. PARK

Duck Cr.

Gneiss Cr.

Richard's Cr.

N

Maple Cr.

GNEISS CREEK TRAIL

Cougar Creek

MADISON VALLEY

WYOMING

MONTANA

Madison Creek

West Yellowstone

WEST ENTRANCE RD

HIKE 69

DETAIL AREA

TO NORTHERN TRAILHEAD (HIKE 78)

COUGAR CREEK TRAIL

GNEISS CREEK TRAIL

MADISON VALLEY

N

E

W

S

ALSO SEE MAPS ON PAGES 8 • 173

P

WEST ENTRANCE RD

Madison River

TO MADISON

TO WEST YELLOWSTONE

GNEISS CREEK TRAIL
FROM THE MADISON RIVER

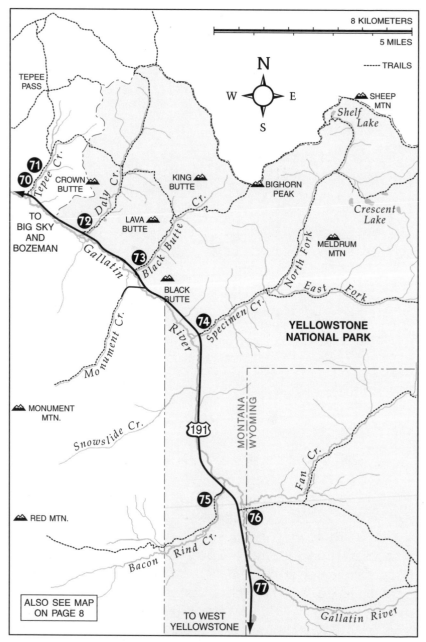

8 KILOMETERS
5 MILES

- - - - TRAILS

N
W   E
S

TEPEE PASS

SHEEP MTN

Shelf Lake

71
70

CROWN BUTTE

Tepee Cr.

Daly Cr.

KING BUTTE

BIGHORN PEAK

Crescent Lake

TO BIG SKY AND BOZEMAN

72

LAVA BUTTE

Black Butte Cr.

Gallatin

73

BLACK BUTTE

MELDRUM MTN

North Fork

East Fork

74

Specimen Cr.

YELLOWSTONE NATIONAL PARK

River

Monument Cr.

MONUMENT MTN.

Snowslide Cr.

191

MONTANA WYOMING

Fan Cr.

RED MTN.

75

76

Bacon Rind Cr.

77

ALSO SEE MAP ON PAGE 8

TO WEST YELLOWSTONE

Gallatin River

HIKES 70–77
GALLATIN VALLEY

Hike 70
Tepee Creek Trail to Tepee Pass

Hiking distance: 6 miles round trip
Hiking time: 3 hours
Elevation gain: 900 feet
Maps: U.S.G.S. Sunshine Point

map
next page

Summary of hike: The Tepee Creek Trail follows up the watercourse of Tepee Creek through expansive grasslands to Tepee Pass at the head of the verdant valley. From the pass are tremendous sweeping views down the wide valley and beyond, from the Madison Range to the Gallatin Range.

Driving directions: From West Yellowstone, drive 33 miles north on Highway 191 (towards Bozeman) to the signed trail on the right by mile marker 32. Turn right and park 100 yards ahead by the trailhead.

From Big Sky, take Highway 191 south for 16 miles to the trailhead on the left.

Hiking directions: Head northeast up the wide grassy draw between Sunshine Point and Crown Butte. Follow the trail along Tepee Creek to a signed junction with the Tepee Creek Cutoff Trail at 1.1 miles. The right fork crosses Tepee Creek and leads eastward into Yellowstone (Hike 71). Take the left fork towards Tepee Pass and Buffalo Horn Divide. Climb a small hill, then traverse the hillside above the valley. Continue past the prominent Grouse Mountain and stands of aspens and pines. After numerous dips and rises along the rolling ridges, the trail begins a half-mile ascent to Tepee Pass. At the top of the valley, near a dense stand of evergreens, is a signed 4-way junction on Tepee Pass. The right fork leads 200 yards to a flat area above the saddle with great views. This is our turnaround spot.

To hike further, the east trail leads two miles to the Yellowstone National Park boundary. From Tepee Pass, a trail descends to the north for 2.5 miles to Buffalo Horn Creek. To the west, a trail leads down Wilson Draw to the Gallatin River.

Hike 71
Tepee Creek Trail to the
Yellowstone National Park boundary

Hiking distance: 4.6 miles round trip
Hiking time: 2.5 hours
Elevation gain: 700 feet
Maps: U.S.G.S. Sunshine Point

Summary of hike: The Tepee Creek Trail begins just outside the northwest corner of Yellowstone National Park. The trail crosses gentle slopes through a broad grassy valley, passing dense tree-lined ridges. The hike ends on a grassy ridgetop at the Yellowstone boundary overlooking the Daly Creek drainage.

Driving directions: From West Yellowstone, drive 33 miles north on Highway 191 (towards Bozeman) to the signed trail on the right by mile marker 32. Turn right and park 100 yards ahead by the trailhead.

From Big Sky, take Highway 191 south for 16 miles to the trailhead on the left.

Hiking directions: Hike northeast past the hitching posts, and cross the grassy slopes along the base of Sunshine Point. Follow the open expanse along the west side of Tepee Creek to a signed junction with the Tepee Creek Cutoff Trail at 1.1 miles. The left fork heads north to Tepee Pass and Buffalo Horn Creek (Hike 70). Take the right fork across Tepee Creek, and continue up the hillside on the east side of the creek. The trail curves to the right and heads east up a narrow drainage surrounded by mountains and tree groves. Near the top of a meadow, follow the ridge to the signed Yellowstone boundary on the saddle. Just below the saddle is a pond. Return to the trailhead the way you came.

To hike further, the trail descends into Yellowstone to Daly Creek (Hike 72).

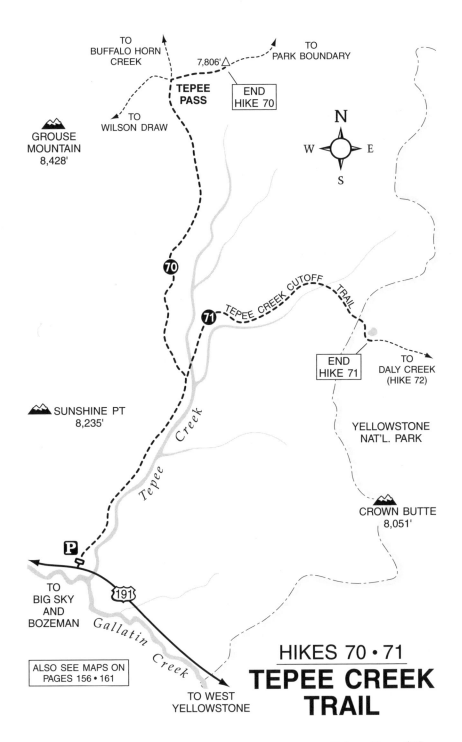

TO
BUFFALO HORN
CREEK

TO
PARK BOUNDARY

7,806'

TEPEE
PASS

END
HIKE 70

TO
WILSON DRAW

N

W   E

S

GROUSE
MOUNTAIN
8,428'

70

71

TEPEE CREEK CUTOFF TRAIL

END
HIKE 71

TO
DALY CREEK
(HIKE 72)

SUNSHINE PT
8,235'

YELLOWSTONE
NAT'L. PARK

Tepee Creek

CROWN BUTTE
8,051'

P

TO
BIG SKY
AND
BOZEMAN

191

Gallatin Creek

ALSO SEE MAPS ON
PAGES 156 • 161

TO WEST
YELLOWSTONE

HIKES 70 • 71
**TEPEE CREEK
TRAIL**

Hike 72
Daly Creek Trail

Hiking distance: 5.2 miles round trip
Hiking time: 2.5 hours
Elevation gain: 350 feet
Maps: U.S.G.S. Sunshine Point and Big Horn Peak
       Trails Illustrated Mammoth Hot Springs

Summary of hike: Daly Creek is the northernmost drainage in Yellowstone National Park. This backcountry hike makes a gradual ascent up the scenic valley, crossing the rolling meadows and open hillsides parallel to Daly Creek. The hillsides are fringed with aspens and Douglas fir. The impressive Crown Butte, Lava Butte, and King Butte formations are prominent throughout the hike. To the northeast is the Sky Rim Ridge.

Driving directions: From West Yellowstone, drive 31.4 miles north on Highway 191 (towards Bozeman) to the signed trail on the right between mile markers 30 and 31. Turn right and park in the lot.

From Big Sky, take Highway 191 south for 17.6 miles to the trailhead on the left.

Hiking directions: Head northeast, skirting around the right side of the embankment parallel to Daly Creek. At a quarter mile, cross the log footbridge over Daly Creek. To the north, on the Yellowstone Park boundary, is the Crown Butte formation. King Butte rises high in the northeast. Climb the rolling ridge along the east side of the drainage through stands of lodgepole pines. Watch for a vernal pool on the right. At one mile, the trail climbs a small hill and crosses a couple of streams to a great profile view of Crown Butte, now to the west. Continue through the open meadows past a signed junction with the Black Butte Cutoff Trail on the right at 1.8 miles. The well-defined trail straight ahead reaches the Tepee Creek Cutoff Trail junction at 2.6 miles. This is the turnaround point.

To hike further, there are two options. To the north, the trail

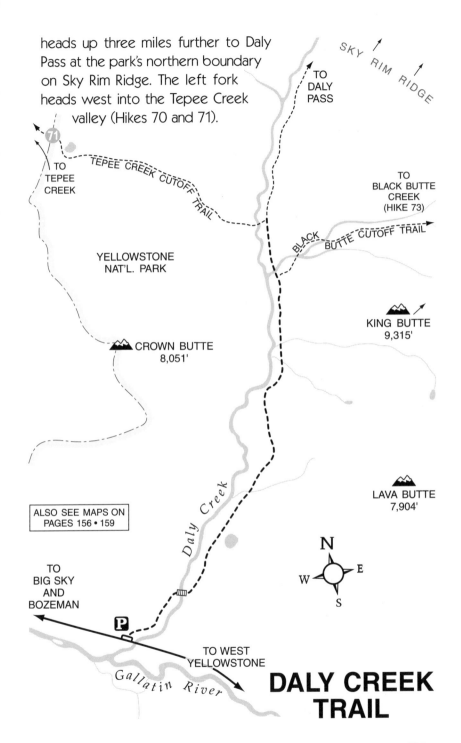

heads up three miles further to Daly Pass at the park's northern boundary on Sky Rim Ridge. The left fork heads west into the Tepee Creek valley (Hikes 70 and 71).

SKY RIM RIDGE

TO DALY PASS

TO TEPEE CREEK

TEPEE CREEK CUTOFF TRAIL

TO BLACK BUTTE CREEK (HIKE 73)

BLACK BUTTE CUTOFF TRAIL

YELLOWSTONE NAT'L. PARK

KING BUTTE 9,315'

CROWN BUTTE 8,051'

LAVA BUTTE 7,904'

ALSO SEE MAPS ON PAGES 156 • 159

Daly Creek

N
W   E
S

TO BIG SKY AND BOZEMAN

P

TO WEST YELLOWSTONE

Gallatin River

DALY CREEK TRAIL

Hike 73
Black Butte Creek Trail

Hiking distance: 4 miles round trip
Hiking time: 2 hours
Elevation gain: 600 feet
Maps: U.S.G.S. Big Horn Peak
       Trails Illustrated Mammoth Hot Springs

Summary of hike: The Black Butte Creek Trail begins at the base of Black Butte in the Gallatin Valley. The trail parallels Black Butte Creek up a beautiful forested drainage to a meadow at the base of King Butte. The narrow valley has aspen, lodgepole pine, and Douglas fir. This trail is an access route up to Big Horn Peak, Shelf Lake, and the summit of Sheep Mountain.

Driving directions: From West Yellowstone, drive 29.8 miles north on Highway 191 towards Bozeman to the signed trail on the right, between mile markers 28 and 29. Park in the parking area on the left, 50 yards south of the signed trail.

From Big Sky, take Highway 191 south for 19.2 miles to the parking area on the right.

Hiking directions: Cross the highway to the signed trail on the north side of Black Butte Creek. Hike up the forested draw between Black Butte and Lava Butte. Head gradually uphill, following the creek through meadows and pine groves along the creek drainage. Meander across the various slopes and rolling hills while remaining close to Black Butte Creek. At 1.5 miles, the trail enters a dense, old growth lodgepole forest. After a quarter-mile, the path breaks out into an open meadow. King Butte and Big Horn Peak tower above to the northeast. At two miles, in the meadow at the base of King Butte, is a signed trail junction. This is the turnaround spot.

To hike further, the left fork leads 2.1 miles to Daly Creek (Hike 72). The right fork crosses the meadow along Black Butte Creek. After crossing the creek, the trail begins a steep ascent to the summit of Bighorn Peak and on to Shelf Lake.

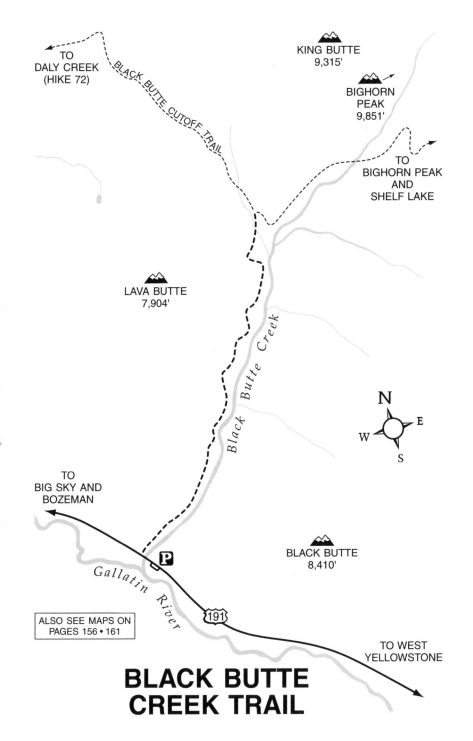

TO
DALY CREEK
(HIKE 72)

BLACK BUTTE CUTOFF TRAIL

KING BUTTE
9,315'

BIGHORN
PEAK
9,851'

TO
BIGHORN PEAK
AND
SHELF LAKE

LAVA BUTTE
7,904'

Black Butte Creek

N
E
W
S

TO
BIG SKY AND
BOZEMAN

P

BLACK BUTTE
8,410'

Gallatin River

191

ALSO SEE MAPS ON
PAGES 156 • 161

TO WEST
YELLOWSTONE

BLACK BUTTE
CREEK TRAIL

Hike 74
Specimen Creek Trail

Hiking distance: 4.2 miles round trip
Hiking time: 2 hours
Elevation gain: 240 feet
Maps: U.S.G.S. Big Horn Peak
        Trails Illustrated Mammoth Hot Springs

Summary of hike: The nearly flat Specimen Creek Trail follows Specimen Creek up the canyon through a mature forest dominated by lodgepole pines. This beautiful drainage crosses bridges over feeder streams to an open meadow at the confluence of the North Fork and East Fork of Specimen Creek. The meadow is frequented by elk and moose.

Driving directions: From West Yellowstone, drive 27.5 miles north on Highway 191 (towards Bozeman) to the signed trail on the right between mile markers 26 and 27. Turn right and park by the trailhead 30 yards ahead.

From Big Sky, take Highway 191 south for 21.5 miles to the trailhead on the left.

Hiking directions: Head east along Specimen Creek through the lodgepole pine forest. Pass talus slopes on the northern side of the narrow drainage. As the canyon widens, the trail alternates between lush stands of pines and open meadows. At 1.3 miles, cross a footbridge over a stream. Traverse the forested hillside to another footbridge over a stream to a signed trail split at two miles. The right fork follows the Sportsman Lake Trail to High Lake and Sportsman Lake, 6 and 8 miles ahead. Take the Specimen Creek Trail to the left. Within minutes is campsite WE1. The campsite sits in an open meadow by Specimen Creek, which meanders through the meadow. A short distance ahead is the confluence of the North Fork and the East Fork. This is our turnaround spot.

To hike further, the trail continues up to the headwaters of the North Fork at Crescent Lake and Shelf Lake.

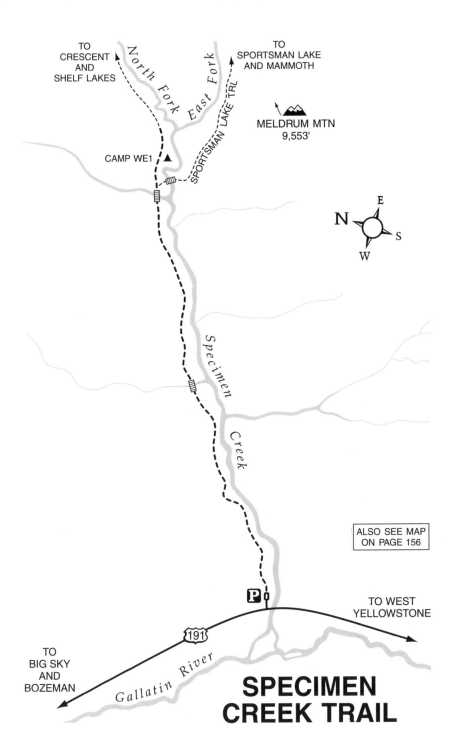

TO
CRESCENT
AND
SHELF LAKES

TO
SPORTSMAN LAKE
AND MAMMOTH

North Fork

East Fork

SPORTSMAN LAKE TRL

MELDRUM MTN
9,553'

CAMP WE1

Specimen

Creek

N
E
S
W

ALSO SEE MAP
ON PAGE 156

P

TO WEST
YELLOWSTONE

191

TO
BIG SKY
AND
BOZEMAN

Gallatin River

SPECIMEN
CREEK TRAIL

Hike 75
Bacon Rind Creek Trail

Hiking distance: 4.2 miles round trip
Hiking time: 2 hours
Elevation gain: 200 feet
Maps: U.S.G.S. Divide Lake
Trails Illustrated Mammoth Hot Springs

Summary of hike: The Bacon Rind Creek Trail is the only hike inside Yellowstone that heads west from the Gallatin Valley. The flat, easy trail parallels the meandering Bacon Rind Creek through a valley surrounded by high mountain peaks. Moose, elk, and grizzly bears frequent the meadow. Beyond the western park boundary, the trail enters the Lee Metcalf Wilderness in the Gallatin National Forest.

Driving directions: From West Yellowstone, drive 23.5 miles north on Highway 191 (towards Bozeman) to the trailhead sign on the left between mile markers 22 and 23. Turn left on the unpaved road, and drive 0.3 miles to the trailhead parking area.

From Big Sky, take Highway 191 south for 25.5 miles to the trailhead turnoff on the right.

Hiking directions: Head south past the trail sign along the north side of Bacon Rind Creek. Follow the drainage upstream through beautiful stands of pines and fir. The path remains close to the riparian watercourse for the first 0.7 miles, where the valley opens to the Gallatin River. Bacon Rind Creek flows placidly through the wide valley between the forested hillsides. Continue up the draw to the head of the valley and cross a stream. Evergreens enclose the top of the meadow at the signed Yellowstone National Park boundary. This is the turn-around point. To return, reverse your route.

To hike further, the trail enters the Lee Metcalf Wilderness, crosses Migration Creek, and eventually ascends to Monument Mountain.

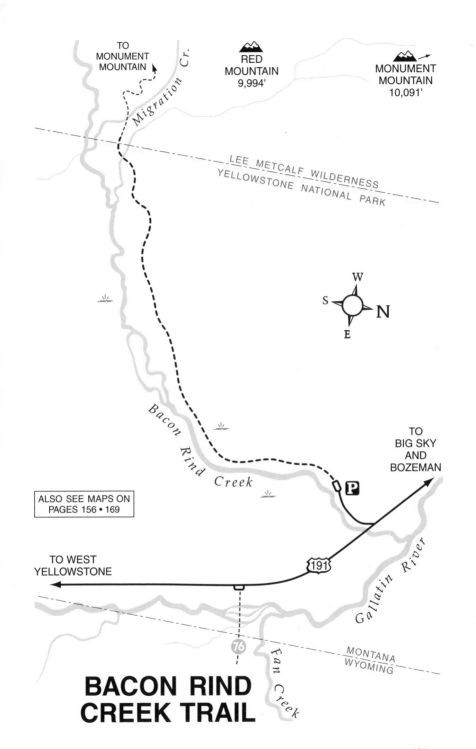

TO
MONUMENT
MOUNTAIN

Migration Cr.

RED
MOUNTAIN
9,994'

MONUMENT
MOUNTAIN
10,091'

LEE METCALF WILDERNESS
YELLOWSTONE NATIONAL PARK

W

S · N

E

Bacon Rind Creek

TO
BIG SKY
AND
BOZEMAN

P

ALSO SEE MAPS ON
PAGES 156 • 169

TO WEST
YELLOWSTONE

191

Gallatin River

76

Fan Creek

MONTANA
WYOMING

BACON RIND
CREEK TRAIL

Hike 76
Fawn Pass Trail to Fan Creek

Hiking distance: 3 miles round trip
Hiking time: 1.5 hours
Elevation gain: 200 feet
Maps: U.S.G.S. Divide Lake
  Trails Illustrated Mammoth Hot Springs

Summary of hike: The Fawn Pass Trail to Fan Creek is an easy hike through forested rolling hills and scenic meadows. The Fan Creek Trail (not shown on the U.S.G.S. map) is a fishing access trail established in the early 1980s. From the junction with the Fawn Pass Trail, the Fan Creek Trail heads northeast along the creek through Fan Creek meadow. Moose and elk frequent this beautiful meadow.

Driving directions: From West Yellowstone, drive 22.8 miles north on Highway 191 (towards Bozeman) to the signed trail on the right, just south of mile marker 22. Turn right and park in the trailhead parking area.

From Big Sky, take Highway 191 south for 26.2 miles to the trailhead on the left.

Hiking directions: Head east down a short flight of steps on the Fawn Pass Trail. After the trail register, cross the meadow marbled with meandering streams that form the upper Gallatin River. A series of wooden footbridges cross the various lucid streams. Ascend the slope and enter the forested hillside. Cross the gently rolling hills to a signed trail split at 1.4 miles. The Fawn Pass Trail bears right to the Bighorn Pass Cutoff Trail and Fawn Pass. Take the Fan Creek Trail to the left. The trail descends into the wide open meadow to Fan Creek. At the creek is a wonderful picnic spot and place to rest.

To hike further, the trail follows Fan Creek through the mountain valley to the Sportsman Lake Trail, wading across Fan Creek three times.

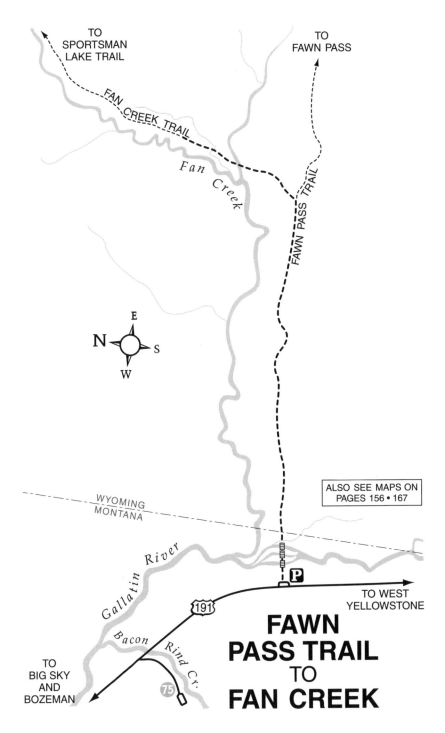

TO
SPORTSMAN
LAKE TRAIL

TO
FAWN PASS

FAN CREEK TRAIL

Fan Creek

FAWN PASS TRAIL

N E S W

WYOMING
MONTANA

ALSO SEE MAPS ON
PAGES 156 • 167

Gallatin River

P

TO WEST
YELLOWSTONE

191

Bacon Rind Cr.

75

TO
BIG SKY
AND
BOZEMAN

FAWN PASS TRAIL TO FAN CREEK

Hike 77
Bighorn Pass Trail
along the Upper Gallatin River

Hiking distance: 1 to 12 miles round trip
Hiking time: Variable
Elevation gain: 150 feet
Maps: U.S.G.S. Divide Lake and Joseph Peak
    Trails Illustrated Mammoth Hot Springs

Summary of hike: The Upper Gallatin Valley is a vast, open meadow that stretches along the Upper Gallatin River for many miles, giving you the option of choosing your own hiking distance. The relaxing hike through the scenic, treeless valley offers excellent trout fishing and wildlife viewing. The trail eventually leads over Bighorn Pass, which can be seen looming in the distance at the end of the valley.

Driving directions: From West Yellowstone, drive 21.3 miles north on Highway 191 (towards Bozeman) to the signed trail on the right between mile markers 20 and 21. Turn right and drive 0.2 miles to the parking area.

From Big Sky, take Highway 191 south for 27.7 miles to the trailhead on the left.

Hiking directions: Take the trail southeast past the hitching posts and trail sign along the west edge of the Gallatin River. Walk through the stands of lodgepole pines, heading upstream along the winding river. At a quarter mile, cross the log bridge over the river. After crossing, continue southeast on the well-defined path. Follow the river through the broad grassy meadows, and enjoy spectacular views of the Gallatin Valley stretching to the east. Turn around at any point along the trail. Bighorn Pass is 12 miles from the trailhead.

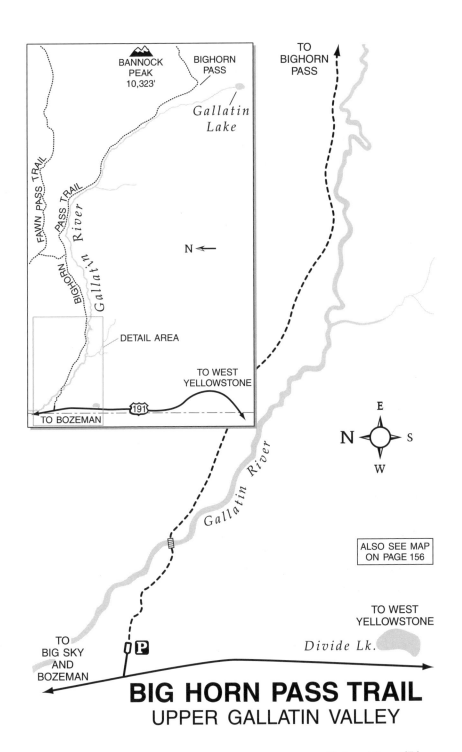

BANNOCK
PEAK
10,323'

BIGHORN
PASS

TO
BIGHORN
PASS

*Gallatin
Lake*

FAWN PASS TRAIL

PASS TRAIL

BIGHORN

Gallatin River

N ←

DETAIL AREA

TO WEST
YELLOWSTONE

191

TO BOZEMAN

Gallatin River

E
N ⊕ S
W

ALSO SEE MAP
ON PAGE 156

TO WEST
YELLOWSTONE

Divide Lk.

TO
BIG SKY
AND
BOZEMAN

P

BIG HORN PASS TRAIL
UPPER GALLATIN VALLEY

Hike 78
Gneiss Creek Trail
from the Gallatin

Hiking distance: 3.6 miles round trip
Hiking time: 2 hours
Elevation gain: 300 feet
Maps: U.S.G.S. Richards Creek
       Trails Illustrated Mammoth Hot Springs

Summary of hike: This hike follows the first portion of the Gneiss Creek Trail from the northwest trailhead in the Gallatin. The 14-mile trail leads through the Madison Valley, crossing several creeks en route to the southern trailhead at the Madison River bridge (see map for Hike 69). This hike is an easy walk through the beautiful open terrain to Campanula Creek, a tributary of Gneiss Creek. The valley is abundant with wildlife.

Driving directions: From West Yellowstone, drive 10.6 miles north on Highway 191 (towards Bozeman) to the signed trail on the right between mile markers 9 and 10. It is by the Fir Ridge Cemetery. Turn right and park in the parking area.

    From Big Sky, take Highway 191 south for 38.4 miles to the trailhead on the left.

Hiking directions: Follow the old, grassy two-track road east through aspen and pine groves. Cross a small rise and parallel the signed Yellowstone Park boundary. At 0.3 miles, the trail enters the park at a sign-in register. Continue along the ridge above Duck Creek and Richards Creek to the south. Head east along the rolling hills spotted with pines and aspens. The trail gradually loses elevation past the forested slopes of Sandy Butte to the right. At the east end of Sandy Butte, descend into the draw to Campanula Creek. Follow the creek upstream a short distance to the creek crossing, the turnaround point for this hike. Return along the same path.

    To hike further, cross the creek and continue southeast through the open, flat valley along Gneiss Creek (see Hike 69).

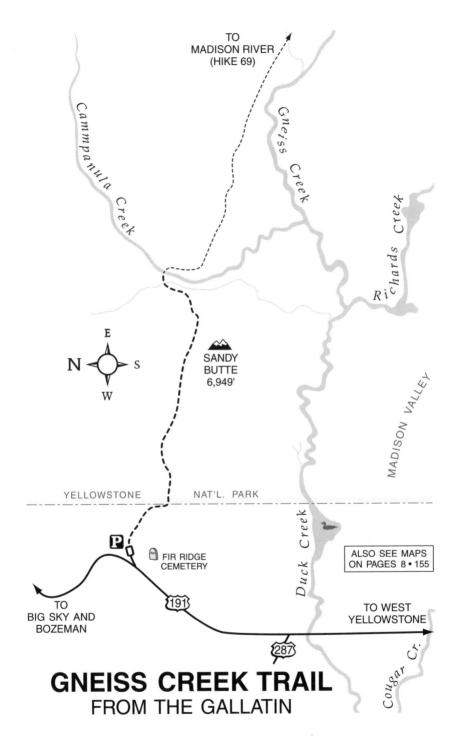

TO
MADISON RIVER
(HIKE 69)

Cammpanula Creek

Gneiss Creek

Richards Creek

E
N W S
W

SANDY
BUTTE
6,949'

Richards Creek

MADISON VALLEY

YELLOWSTONE   NAT'L. PARK

Duck Creek

P

FIR RIDGE
CEMETERY

ALSO SEE MAPS
ON PAGES 8 • 155

TO
BIG SKY AND
BOZEMAN

191

TO WEST
YELLOWSTONE

287

Cougar Cr.

GNEISS CREEK TRAIL
FROM THE GALLATIN

Hike 79
Red Canyon Trail

Hiking distance: 2 miles round trip
Hiking time: 1 hour
Elevation gain: 500 feet
Maps: U.S.G.S. Mount Hebgen
       Madison and Gallatin Rivers Fishing and Hunting map

Summary of hike: The Red Canyon Trail leads to the Cabin Creek Wildlife Management Area of the Lee Metcalf Wilderness. The trail follows Red Canyon Creek past the Red Canyon Fault, a 20-foot break on the southern slopes of Kirkwood Ridge. The fault was created in 1959 during the Madison River Canyon earthquake. Near Kirkwood Ridge are scenic views back down the canyon.

Driving directions: From downtown West Yellowstone, drive 8 miles north on Highway 191 towards Bozeman. Turn left on Highway 287 towards Ennis. At 4.6 miles, turn right onto Red Canyon Road (marked with a Forest Service sign). Drive up Red Canyon Road 2.7 miles to the trailhead at road's end and park.

Hiking directions: Head north on the well-defined path along the west side of Red Canyon Creek through a forest of lodgepole pine and Engelmann spruce. The prominent Kirkwood Ridge, with its sculpted limestone formations, towers above the trail to the northwest. At a quarter mile is a trail split. The right fork leads a short distance to the Red Canyon Fault. The main trail follows the left fork and ascends the hillside out of the lush drainage. Switchbacks lead up and across the open forest along the faultline. Continue gently up the draw, reaching a large, rolling meadow with wildflowers at one mile. There are great views back down Red Canyon to Hebgen Lake. This is the turnaround spot.

To hike further, the trail climbs alongside Red Canyon Creek in the Cabin Creek Wildlife Management Area and connects with the Tepee Creek Trail.

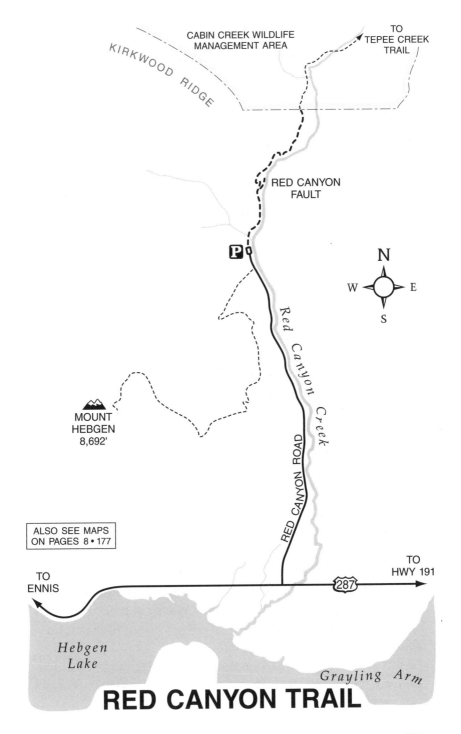

KIRKWOOD RIDGE

CABIN CREEK WILDLIFE
MANAGEMENT AREA

TO
TEPEE CREEK
TRAIL

RED CANYON
FAULT

P

N

W — E

S

Red Canyon Creek

MOUNT
HEBGEN
8,692'

RED CANYON ROAD

ALSO SEE MAPS
ON PAGES 8 • 177

TO
ENNIS

TO
HWY 191

287

*Hebgen
Lake*

Grayling Arm

RED CANYON TRAIL

Hike 80
Horse Butte Lookout
HORSE BUTTE PENINSULA

Hiking distance: 3.4 miles round trip
Hiking time: 2 hours
Elevation gain: 500 feet
Maps: U.S.G.S. Madison Arm and Mount Hebgen
　　　　Madison and Gallatin Rivers Fishing and Hunting map

Summary of hike: Horse Butte Peninsula stretches into Hebgen Lake just west of Yellowstone National Park. The peninsula lies between the Madison Arm and the Grayling Arm of Hebgen Lake in a basin south of the Gallatin National Forest's rugged mountains. It is a vital wildlife corridor with a wide diversity of plants. Horse Butte Lookout is a fire tower that sits 450 feet above the lake. This uphill trail follows an unpaved road through open meadows with wildflowers and an old-growth Douglas fir forest. From the lookout are views of the Madison Arm, Hebgen Lake, Edwards Peninsula, Yellowstone National Park, and the Continental Divide. It is an excellent bird-watching location to spot bald eagles, osprey, and pelicans.

Driving directions: From downtown West Yellowstone, drive 5 miles north on Highway 191 towards Bozeman. Turn left at Rainbow Point Road. Turn left again 3.2 miles ahead at a four-way junction. Continue 1.6 miles to Horse Butte Lookout Road. The road, which is marked, forks to the right. This lightly used vehicle road is the hiking trail. Park anywhere along the side of the road.

Hiking directions: Hike northwest, curving up the unpaved road. As the elevation increases, views continuously open to Hebgen Lake and the Madison Arm. At 1.3 miles the trail enters an old growth forest for a quarter mile. At the top, the trail curves around the hilltop meadow to the fire lookout and picnic area. It is a great place to have lunch and marvel at the beautiful views. Return along the same route.

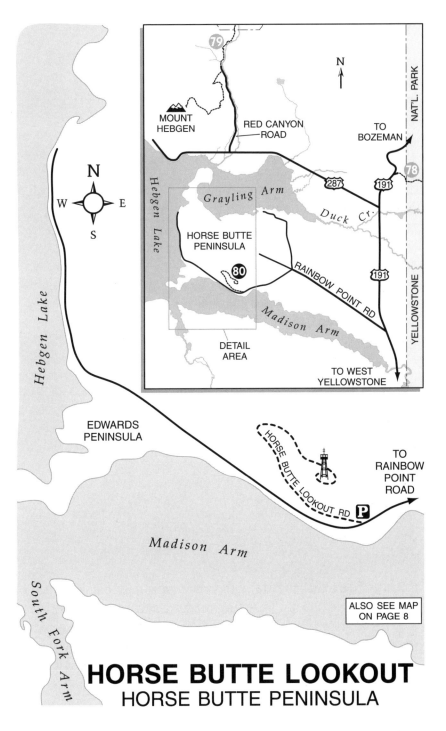

HORSE BUTTE LOOKOUT
HORSE BUTTE PENINSULA

Hike 81
Riverside Trail

Hiking distance: 5 miles round trip
Hiking time: 2.5 hours
Elevation gain: Level
Maps: U.S.G.S. West Yellowstone
Trails Illustrated Old Faithful or Mammoth Hot Springs

Summary of hike: The Riverside Trail is an easy river stroll along the banks of the Madison River. The trail begins in the town of West Yellowstone and immediately enters Yellowstone National Park. The path leads through a lodgepole pine forest to the flats along the Madison River. At the river are views of Mount Holmes and the Gallatin Mountain Range. In the morning, it is common to see moose along the river banks. During the winter, it is a popular cross-country ski trail.

Driving directions: In West Yellowstone, drive to the intersection of Madison Avenue and Boundary Street, which cross two blocks east of downtown. Park along Boundary Street.

A second access to the Madison River is located a half mile from the west entrance station inside Yellowstone. A one-mile road leads northeast to a parking area.

Hiking directions: From the east side of Boundary Street, walk through the opening in the pole fence at the signed trailhead, directly across from Madison Avenue. The fence is the west boundary of Yellowstone National Park. Head east through the lodgepole pine forest to the powerlines. Follow the wide path beneath the powerpoles to a junction at a half mile. The right fork heads south to the west park entrance station. Continue straight ahead to the east, reaching a T-junction with a gravel road at 1.1 miles. Cross the road and take the gated road straight ahead. Descend to the banks of the Madison River, and meader upstream to the right along the southwest river bank. Pass a stream gaging station, where the road narrows to a footpath. The trail ends at a pullout from the park road that overlooks the river. Return 0.8 miles to the T-junction with the gravel road. Follow the road downstream and head north to a Y-fork. The right fork ends at a picnic area on the river bank. The left fork continues 0.4 miles to a ledge above the river.

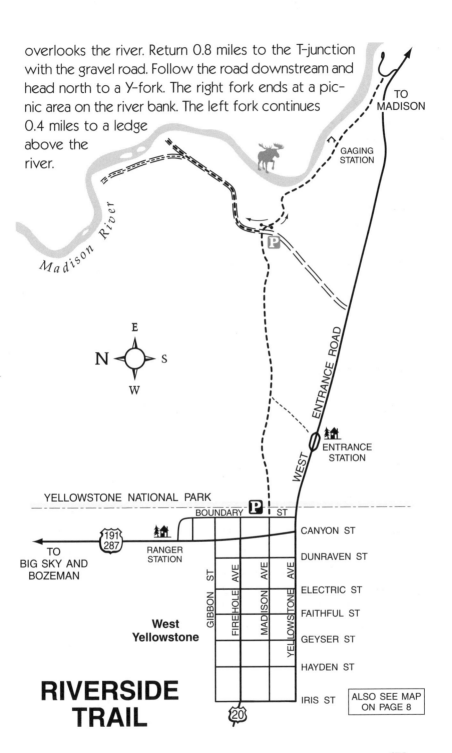

TO MADISON

GAGING STATION

WEST ENTRANCE ROAD

ENTRANCE STATION

YELLOWSTONE NATIONAL PARK

BOUNDARY ST

CANYON ST

DUNRAVEN ST

ELECTRIC ST

FAITHFUL ST

GEYSER ST

HAYDEN ST

IRIS ST

191 287

TO BIG SKY AND BOZEMAN

RANGER STATION

West Yellowstone

GIBBON ST

FIREHOLE AVE

MADISON AVE

YELLOWSTONE AVE

20

RIVERSIDE TRAIL

Madison River

E
N — S
W

ALSO SEE MAP ON PAGE 8

Hike 82
Targhee Creek Trail

Hiking distance: 5 miles round trip
Hiking time: 2.5 hours
Elevation gain: 250 feet
Maps: U.S.G.S. Targhee Pass and Targhee Peak, Idaho
    U.S.F.S. Gallatin National Forest—West Half
    Madison and Gallatin Rivers Fishing and Hunting map

Summary of hike: The Targhee Creek Trail parallels Targhee Creek to alpine Clark and Edwards Lakes near the headwaters of the creek. The trail follows the drainage between Targhee Peak to the west and Bald Peak to the east near the Continental Divide. This hike meanders up the first 2.5 miles of the canyon along Targhee Creek through meadows and pine forests. Throughout the hike, Targhee Peak rises like a monolith high above the trail.

Driving directions: From downtown West Yellowstone, drive 11.4 miles on Highway 20 towards Idaho. Turn right at the signed Targhee Creek Trails. Drive one mile to the well-marked trailhead and park.

Hiking directions: From the parking area, head north past the trail sign towards the prominent Targhee Peak. The trail strolls gently up the drainage through pine forests, open hillsides, and rolling meadows. At 2.5 miles, a footbridge crosses over to the west side of Targhee Creek. This is our turnaround spot.

To hike further, the trail continues up the canyon, reaching Clark Lake at 6.5 miles while gaining an additional 1,800 feet in elevation.

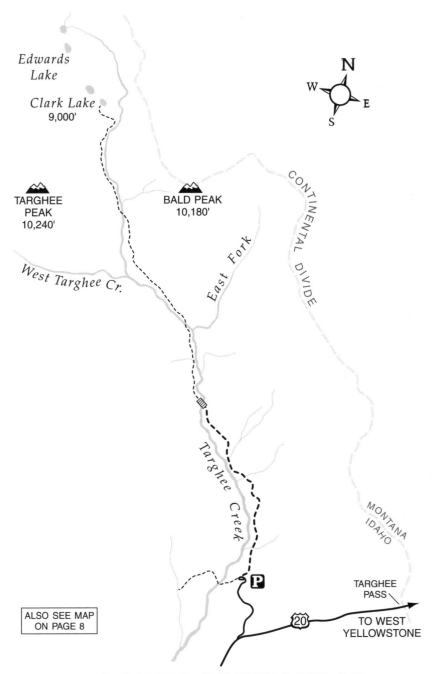

Edwards Lake

Clark Lake
9,000'

TARGHEE
PEAK
10,240'

West Targhee Cr.

BALD PEAK
10,180'

East Fork

CONTINENTAL DIVIDE

N
W   E
S

Targhee Creek

P

ALSO SEE MAP
ON PAGE 8

MONTANA
IDAHO

TARGHEE
PASS

20

TO WEST
YELLOWSTONE

TARGHEE CREEK TRAIL

DAY HIKE BOOKS

Day Hikes In Yellowstone National Park ....1-57342-048-4 ....$12.95

Day Hikes In Grand Teton National Park ....1-57342-046-8 ....11.95

Day Hikes In the Beartooth Mountains
Red Lodge, MT to Yellowstone Nat'l. Park ....1-57342-034-4 ....11.95

Day Hikes Around Bozeman, Montana ....1-57342-033-6 ....11.95

Day Hikes Around Missoula, Montana ....1-57342-032-8 ....11.95

Day Hikes In Sequoia and
Kings Canyon Nat'l. Parks ....1-57342-030-1 ....12.95

Day Hikes In Yosemite National Park ....1-57342-037-9 ....11.95

Day Hikes On the California Central Coast ....1-57342-031-X 14.95

Day Hikes On the California Southern Coast ....1-57342-045-X 14.95

Day Hikes Around Monterey and Carmel ....1-57342-036-0 ....14.95

Day Hikes Around Big Sur ....1-57342-041-7 ....14.95

Day Hikes In San Luis Obispo County ....1-57342-022-0 ....14.95

Day Hikes Around Santa Barbara ....1-57342-042-5 ....14.95

Day Hikes Around Ventura County ....1-57342-043-3 ....14.95

Day Hikes Around Los Angeles ....1-57342-044-1 ....14.95

Day Hikes Around Orange County ....1-57342-047-6 ....15.95

Day Hikes Around Sedona, Arizona ....1-57342-049-2 ....14.95

Day Hikes On Oahu ....1-57342-038-7 ....11.95

Day Hikes On Maui ....1-57342-039-5 ....11.95

Day Hikes On Kauai ....1-57342-040-9 ....11.95

These books may be purchased at your local bookstore or
outdoor shop. Or, order them direct from the distributor:

The Globe Pequot Press

246 Goose Lane • P.O. Box 480 • Guilford, CT 06437-0480
on the web: www.globe-pequot.com

800-243-0495 DIRECT **800-820-2329** FAX

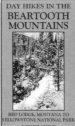

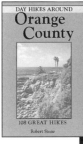
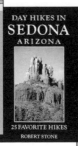

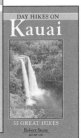

Notes

About the Author

For more than a decade, veteran hiker Robert Stone has been writer, photographer, and publisher of Day Hike Books. Robert has hiked every trail in the *Day Hike Book* series. With 21 hiking guides in the series, many in their second, third, and fourth editions, he has hiked thousands of miles of trails throughout the western United States and Hawaii. When Robert is not hiking, he researches, writes, and maps the hikes before returning to the trails. He spends summers in the Rocky Mountains of Montana and winters on the California Central Coast.